ALWAYS BE LISTENING

SUPERCHARGE YOUR SALES BY LISTENING MORE & CLOSING LESS

By

DAVE INGLAND

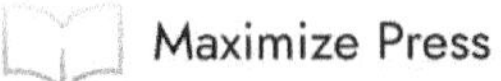

Maximize Press

ISBN-13: 979-8-9888124-0-1 (Paperback)
ISBN-13: 979-8-9888124-1-8 (Hardcover)

First edition 2023

Maximize Press - www.maximizepress.com

ALWAYS BE LISTENING

ACKNOWLEDGMENTS

Committing the time to gather my thoughts and write this book has taken more than a decade. Once I sat down to start the writing process, it took about three months, when I thought it would only take about two weeks. From all my years of working in the automotive industry and gaining the experience to share my story, to the months of being alone in my office with my computer, I want to express my gratitude to my wife, Charlotte, for allowing me the opportunity to complete this project and for her encouragement, patience, and support in seeing it through. Thank you, my dear!

I am eternally grateful to my daughters, Megan and Samantha, who were always there for me, and gave me the space I required to make this book a reality. I love you both very much.

I have spent over 15 years as an automotive sales professional and a general sales manager. It has had many ups and downs, rewards and sacrifices. Without being given my first opportunity to be promoted to sales management by Ed Matthews, none of this would have been possible. I owe my ability to compile all of my experiences into this book thanks to your trust and belief in me and my abilities. Thank you, Ed.

To my friends who have been with me since our days together in Oxnard, CA: Claudia, Elizabeth, TJ, Victor, Jose, Reyna, Arely, Ashley, Max, Alisha, Marissa, Jen, Doug, Arthur, Christian, Jenn, Adi, Maggy, Shawna. Thomas, and the team that helped shape my early years from an internet salesperson to a sales manager, I owe you a lifetime of gratitude. Special thanks to my two lifelong friends, Anthony Huerta and Steve Garcia. You've been with me through everything, and I have watched you grow in your dealership responsibilities and as human beings. I am a better human because of the influence you have had on my life. Thanks for everything.

Many thanks to my team in Santa Monica, CA, that allowed me to continue to grow my influence and rewarded me with the achievements you all made after life moved us on to our next chapters. To Nina, Art, Morgan, Anne, Ronnie, Adam, Ferdinand, Sean Hornbeck, and Tommy Hsu, thanks for staying connected with me all these years.

Kaitlin, Angel, and Mark, thanks for making our time together in a tough situation so much better by being positive influences and compassionate during a rough season. I am grateful to have the chance to continue sharing life together long-distance. Thanks for the positive memories of our time together in Colorado.

To Rae Selvey, who was instrumental in my knowledge and understanding of this business and took the time to mentor and prepare me for what was to come, and to Christine for being such a great person to work with and allowing me to be your teammate, many thanks to you. Thanks to Cyndi for always keeping my spirits up when the skies were dark gray and rainy and to Jeremy and Sam for your support and encouragement. Special thanks to my brothers Oscar and JT – thanks for making work, and life, so much fun. Thank you as well to Carlos Martinez, who inspired me to do my best and gave me hope of a brighter future in this business. Your inspiration to learn the business and become a leader in this industry kept me going when things weren't happening as fast as I had hoped for. I owe you a big debt and appreciate all that you did for me. My time with all of you in Portland prepared me to be successful when I moved to Los Angeles, the largest and most competitive automobile market in the United States.

My teams here in San Francisco have become the recipients of all of the hard work my previous teams have endured for the sake of success and has allowed us to become great partners and friends. To everyone here with me going through all of the highs and lows of the market in the past few years: Steven Gu, Thomas, Sophia Wong, Dinu, Jeremy, Eugene, James, Andy Larijani, Seffie, Juanito, Chris Reker, Scott, Josh, Ashur, Devan, Briana, Farshid, Ben, Michelle, Ladd, and Phong Tran, it was during our time together that this book was finally made ready to be written and your successes are part of the story. Thank you friends.

To my amazing BFF's Jessica Cortes Vera, Jocelyn Mieskalski, and Jennypher Dhuyvetter, thank you for keeping me sane and supporting me during this project. We all need a Jessica, Jocelyn, and a Jennypher in our lives and I am so lucky to have all three of you with me. Love, always.

Special thanks to Joe Shaghasi who gave me the opportunity to develop and refine my leadership style and trust in me to advance our teams to achieve our goals — I would never have had the courage to take on a project like this book without you pushing me and making me better. Thanks for your mentorship and friendship over the past 7 years.

To my book production team, thanks for your help in completing the work of turning my story into a finished product: Thank you Tochi Design @tochi_design on Fiverr) for making the color orange work for the book cover. Thank you to my editing team of Nina Grant (@nina_grant on Fiverr) and Talha A (@tulha_abid on Fiverr) for making the book easy to read and a useful reference.

Finally, I want to extend my heartfelt thanks to everyone not mentioned who played a role, no matter how small, in this journey. Your input and influence were invaluable, and I want you all to know how much I appreciate your contributions to the creation of this book.

PREFACE

In a world filled with noise and distractions, the art of truly listening has become a rare and invaluable skill. *Always Be Listening* is a journey into the power of listening – not merely hearing words, but understanding the unspoken, deciphering emotions, and forging deeper connections with those around us.

As I embarked on the path to write this book, I was reminded of the profound impact listening has had on my life. From the early days of my career in the automotive industry to the moments shared with friends and mentors, the ability to listen and comprehend has been a guiding force. Each story, lesson, and insight within these pages reflects the experiences that shaped my understanding of the significance of this skill.

In the pages that follow, we'll delve into the various facets of listening, from active listening techniques to the emotional intelligence that arises when we truly tune in. We'll explore how listening is not limited to professional success, but is equally essential in our personal lives, enriching our relationships and enhancing our interactions with the world.

My aim is for *Always Be Listening* to serve as a guide, offering practical advice, stories, and exercises that can help you harness the power of listening in your own life. I invite you to join me on this journey as we explore the transformative impact of being *Always Listening*. May the insights shared within these pages inspire you to listen not only with your ears but with your heart, and in doing so, empower you to create a world where genuine understanding and authentic connections flourish.

Dave Ingland

v

TABLE OF CONTENTS

INTRODUCTION

In the dynamic realm of automotive sales, the art of conversation holds a pivotal position. But amidst the myriad courses, workshops, and books available on the subject, there's a critical aspect often overlooked: listening. Welcome to *Always Be Listening: Supercharge Your Sales by Listening More & Closing Less,* where we embark on a transformative journey to hone the power of listening as a catalyst for success in automotive sales.

It brings to mind a telling incident during a Friday morning sales meeting I was leading. One salesperson, visibly frustrated, declared, "The internet is going to ruin the car business." Curious, I challenged that person to tell me how many vehicles our dealership sold in a month that were transacted completely online. He was stumped. To shed some light, our dealership at that time sold merely about 5% of its total monthly sales through 100% online transactions.

His outburst wasn't just about the rise of the internet; it was a manifestation of his deeper fears. He had witnessed a 50% dip in his sales and was scrambling for reasons. For him, the internet was the villain, siphoning off his opportunities. The reality? Our dealership's numbers painted a different story. The true issue lay in his entrenched "always be closing" mindset, a belief perpetuated by countless sales managers. This belief asserts that a successful salesperson is essentially a well-oiled machine of rehearsed word tracks, ever ready to counter objections. The conventional wisdom? To excel in sales, one must always be on the offensive — always be closing.

If you're reading this book, chances are you've been told countless times to push for the close, to always be selling, or perhaps to adopt certain word tracks to counter objections. It's not your fault. This has been the modus operandi of countless sales training regimens for decades. However, in the modern age, where personal connection is valued over a rehearsed pitch, it's time to revolutionize our approach.

Instead of always trying to speak, what if we flipped the script? What if, by genuinely listening to our customers, we could gain insights, build genuine relationships, and drive sales, not through pressure, but through understanding? This is the core idea behind this book.

Allow me to illustrate this shift with a simple anecdote. Imagine you're at a party. You're talking to someone about a recent trip you took, but you notice they're not really paying attention. They're waiting for their turn to speak, nodding occasionally, and glancing around. Compare that to a conversation where the person is genuinely engrossed in your story, asking relevant questions, and reacting emotionally. Which person would you trust more? Which conversation would you remember?

Now, let's transfer that analogy to the showroom floor. Your customers are people with individual dreams, fears, needs, and desires. By truly listening to them, you'll be better equipped to cater to those needs, and in turn, foster a deeper level of trust and loyalty. This, in essence, is the art of empathetic listening, the bedrock upon which our sales strategy is built.

In the coming chapters, we'll delve deeply into various facets of this skill. Starting with **Chapter 1**, you'll discover the transformative "Power of Listening." From understanding its profound impact on relationships to realizing its role in driving sales, we'll unravel why it's time to put listening at the forefront.

Chapter 2 delves into the "Basics of Communication." As we unravel the nuances of verbal and non-verbal cues, you'll begin to appreciate the layers of every interaction, understanding that effective communication is often more about what isn't said.

With a solid foundation, we then progress to **Chapter 3** where we immerse ourselves in the "Art of Active Listening." It's more than just hearing words; it's about truly comprehending, processing, and responding to them.

By Chapter 4, you'll be well-versed in the dynamics of "Building Rapport Through Listening," understanding that the depth of your connection with clients can directly influence the success of your sales.

As we navigate through **Chapters 5 to 8**, from "Empathetic Listening" to the essential mindset of "Listening to Understand, Not Just to Respond," the lens through which you perceive client interactions will transform. Every conversation becomes an opportunity, a chance to delve deeper, understand more profoundly, and serve better.

Chapter 9 offers invaluable insights into "The Role of Listening in Negotiation." Here, the power of silence, the nuances of pauses, and the strength of affirmation come into sharp focus.

Finally, **Chapter 10** emphasizes "Cultivating a Listening Mindset," providing you with tools, habits, and practices to ensure that empathetic listening isn't just a strategy but becomes an intrinsic part of your sales persona.

After exploring the foundational concepts in the initial chapters, we're not stopping there. Included in the book are five bonus chapters that further deepen our understanding of the listening paradigm:

Chapter 11, "Storytelling and Sales: Listening to Craft a Narrative," explores how listening can shape compelling stories that resonate with customers.

Chapter 12, "Trade-ins and Upgrades: Listening to Evolving Needs," demonstrates the importance of understanding the changing desires of customers.

Chapter 13, "Bridging the Generation Gap: Listening Across Ages," offers strategies to communicate effectively with diverse age groups, leveraging listening as a unifying tool.

Chapter 14, "Word Tracks vs Authentic Dialogue," challenges traditional scripted interactions, advocating for genuine conversations anchored in deep listening.

Chapter 15, "The First Impression: Setting the Stage with Attentive Listening," underscores the significance of making impactful first impressions by being present and attuned.

Throughout this book, I've integrated valuable quotes and excerpts from esteemed authors and thought leaders. Their wisdom, intertwined with practical strategies, will equip you to elevate your sales game, forging connections that go beyond mere transactions.

In this era of information overload, it's easy to underestimate the profound power of silence, of pausing, of truly listening. Set, as you will discover, in the realm of sales and beyond, listening might just be the secret weapon we've all been searching for.

To every reader, whether you're a seasoned sales professional or just starting out, let this book be your guide to navigating the complex labyrinth of human interactions. By mastering the art of listening, you're not just improving your sales; you're enriching every relationship and interaction in your life.

Welcome to *Always Be Listening*. Dive in, challenge your preconceptions, and unlock the boundless potential that awaits when you truly start to listen.

CHAPTER ONE

THE POWER OF LISTENING

In today's automotive sales landscape, rife with rapid technological advancements and information at the fingertips of customers, one skill stands out as timelessly potent and consistently transformative — listening. At its core, this simple act transcends transactional dialogues, transforming them into powerful moments of connection and trust. And in these moments, true sales potential is realized.

A Silent Revolution

"Why listen when you can talk?" a young salesperson quipped at one of the many seminars I've attended. Ironically, his statement captures the very essence of a common misconception in sales. The prevailing idea seems to be that talking more, impressing with knowledge, and pushing a narrative are the pillars of a successful sale. But if we step back, we realize that sales isn't just about transferring information; it's about building relationships. And what better way to understand someone, to truly connect with them, than by listening?

"People don't care how much you know until they know how much you care." — Theodore Roosevelt.

This insightful quote by Roosevelt taps into the heart of the matter. Your extensive knowledge about the latest car model's features, its torque, or fuel efficiency, while crucial, takes a backseat when the customer doesn't feel genuinely understood or cared for.

The Foundation of Trust

Imagine two scenarios. In the first, you walk into a dealership, and before you can share your thoughts, a salesperson bombards you with the latest promotions, the awards their car models have won, and a scripted persuasion to make a purchase. In the second scenario, a salesperson greets you, inquires about your needs, listens intently, and responds by aligning their offerings with your expressed desires. In which scenario are you more likely to make a purchase?

The answer is clear. By listening, the salesperson in the second scenario builds trust. When customers feel heard, they feel valued. This trust forms the bedrock of a successful sales strategy. It fosters loyalty, generates word-of-mouth referrals, and, most crucially, encourages the customer to buy.

The Trust Ladder

Picture trust as a ladder. Every rung is a step closer to establishing a solid foundation with a customer. Every interaction, every conversation, and especially every listening moment helps a salesperson ascend this ladder. Conversely, every missed opportunity to listen, every premature or inappropriate sales pitch, and every disregard for the customer's sentiments can send the salesperson plummeting.

At the bottom rung, customers may know you. They see you as just another representative of a brand. By the middle rung, they start understanding that you might have something they need. But at the top, they believe in you. They're convinced not just of the product's value, but more crucially, of your genuine intent to serve their best interests.

Trust is Reciprocal

One of the fundamental principles of human psychology is reciprocity. When someone does something for us, we naturally want to return the favor. Listening, in its purest form, is a gift. When salespeople genuinely listen, they're not just gathering information; they're giving their time, attention, and respect. And customers, sensing this gesture, often reciprocate with trust.

The Ripple Effect of Trust

Trust doesn't operate in a vacuum. It has a ripple effect. A customer who trusts you is more open to your recommendations, more forgiving of minor lapses, and more likely to return for repeat purchases. Additionally, they become ambassadors of trust, sharing their positive experiences with friends and family, thereby amplifying your reach and potential customer base.

Building Trust Through Authenticity

In the digital age, authenticity has become a buzzword. But in the realm of sales, it's a tangible asset. It's not enough to merely act trustworthy; one has to be trustworthy. This involves a commitment to honesty, even when it might not lead to an immediate sale. It might mean advising a customer against a higher-priced car because a lower-priced model better suits their needs. Such moments, where a salesperson places a customer's needs above immediate profits, are gold mines for trust-building.

The Inextricable Link Between Listening and Trust

While there are multiple avenues to build trust, listening remains its most potent catalyst. Listening shows customers that they are not just transactional entities but valued individuals. When a salesperson listens, they hear beyond the words. They grasp the emotions, the concerns, the aspirations, and the hesitations. Addressing these not only enhances the sales process but solidifies trust.

In one study, it was found that patients of doctors who listened were more compliant with medical regimens, felt more satisfied with their care, and had better health outcomes. Translated to automotive sales, customers of salespeople who listen are more likely to be satisfied, loyal, and drive away with a car that truly resonates with their needs.

By anchoring our sales approach in trust and understanding its intricate ties with the act of listening, automotive salespeople can not only enhance their sales numbers but also enrich the very essence of the sales experience. At the heart of every successful transaction lies a relationship built on trust, and at the heart of trust lies the potent act of genuine listening.

Beyond the Words

In the vast landscape of communication, words form just the tip of the iceberg; much of what is communicated resides beneath the surface. This subtlety, laden with emotions, stories, and aspirations, often speaks louder than words. In automotive sales, this subtlety can hold the key to genuinely understanding a customer's needs.

Deciphering the Emotional Undertones

Every customer who steps into a showroom carries with them a myriad of emotions: excitement, apprehension, hope, doubt, and many more. These emotions often manifest in subtle cues—a fleeting hesitation before answering a question, an enthusiastic sparkle in the eyes, or nervous fidgeting. Truly effective listeners don't just hear words; they sense these emotional undertones.

For example, when a parent repeatedly asks about safety features, their primary concern might not just be the technical specifics but an underlying anxiety about their child's safety. Recognizing this emotional layer allows the salesperson to address deeper concerns and provide assurance.

Uncovering Stories

Every purchase has a story. The couple buying an SUV might be preparing for adventurous road trips. The young professional opting for an eco-friendly car may be deeply passionate about sustainability. The elderly gentleman choosing a comfortable sedan might be gifting himself a retirement present.

By listening actively and asking the right questions, salespeople can uncover these stories. Knowing them doesn't just help in guiding customers to the right vehicle but also in personalizing the sales journey, making it memorable.

Recognizing Aspirations

For many, cars are not just vehicles; they are dreams on wheels. The young executive might see in a sports car not just speed but a symbol of her hard-earned success. The environmentally conscious teacher might view a hybrid not just as a car, but as a statement of his values.

When salespeople listen beyond words, they recognize these aspirations. Addressing them transforms the sales narrative from merely selling a car to fulfilling a dream.

The Magic of Genuine Engagement

Leo Buscaglia, in his book *Living, Loving, and Learning*, beautifully captures the essence of genuine human connection: "Too often we underestimate the power of a touch, a smile, a kind word, a listening ear, an honest compliment, or the smallest act of caring, all of which have the potential to turn a life around." This observation rings especially true in sales. When a salesperson offers a genuine compliment about a customer's choice, acknowledges their concerns with empathy, or simply listens with undivided attention, they're not just fostering a sale; they're weaving the fabric of a relationship.

This relationship, built on understanding and genuine care, often transcends the immediate sale. It fosters loyalty, generates word-of-mouth recommendations, and elevates the brand's reputation.

To truly understand and connect with customers, automotive salespeople must train themselves to listen not just with their ears, but with their hearts and intuition. In doing so, they move beyond transactional interactions and step into the realm of transformative sales experiences. This deeper connection not only enhances the likelihood of a sale but also enriches the very essence of the customer-salesperson relationship.

Active Engagement

The sales terrain is rife with challenges, and among the most formidable are customer objections. These can range from concerns about pricing and performance to reservations stemming from past experiences. However, rather than viewing objections as obstacles, it's transformative to see them as opportunities—chances to genuinely engage, understand, and address the concerns of the potential buyer. This reframing can only truly occur when there's active engagement through listening.

Active engagement is not about passive nods or rehearsed responses. It's a dynamic dance of give-and-take, where the salesperson is both a keen listener and a strategic communicator. In this delicate balance, the power of active listening emerges, turning potential resistance into enduring reliance. And in this transformation, salespeople don't just close deals; they open doors to lasting connections.

Creative Problem Solving

One of the fundamental principles of successful sales is anticipation—foreseeing potential roadblocks and navigating around them even before they arise. This is where active listening shines its brightest. By genuinely engaging with customers and listening to their stories, concerns, and desires, salespeople can preemptively tailor their pitches and presentations. Instead of reacting to objections, they're proactively addressing them.

For instance, a family discussing ample trunk space might be hinting at their frequent road trips or outdoor activities. Recognizing this not only allows the salesperson to suggest vehicles catering to this need but also to paint a picture—of spacious trunks packed for weekend getaways, of hassle-free travels, and memorable adventures.

Personalization is Key

It's said that customization enhances commitment. When customers feel that the product or service has been uniquely tailored for them, their investment, both emotional and financial, often deepens. By actively listening to cues, both overt and subtle, salespeople can personalize their approach. Such a bespoke approach not only allays specific concerns but also makes the customer feel singularly valued.

Consider a customer who reminisces about their old convertible. While they might be inquiring about sedans today, this nostalgia is a doorway. A listening salesperson might weave in the joys of convertible drives while discussing the advantages of modern sedans, creating a bridge between past joys and future possibilities.

The Art of Making Customers Feel Seen and Heard

Dale Carnegie, in his seminal book, *How to Win Friends and Influence People*, offers profound wisdom: "Be a good listener. Encourage others to talk about themselves." This isn't merely a strategy; it's an acknowledgment of a basic human need. When people feel heard, they feel significant. In the world of sales, this feeling of significance can often be the pivotal point, tipping the balance from consideration to purchase.

Moreover, when customers feel they are the focal point, not just the potential sale, their trust in the salesperson and the brand solidifies. This isn't merely about making a sale; it's about laying the foundation for a lasting relationship.

The Shift from Persuasion to Perception

Traditionally, sales have been viewed through the lens of persuasion. But listening steers us towards perception. Instead of trying to change a customer's mind, we focus on understanding it. This shift is revolutionary. By aligning our sales pitch with the customer's perception, we move from confrontational selling to collaborative selling.

Conclusion

The power of listening in automotive sales is transformative. It provides us with insights, fosters trust, builds relationships, and, most crucially, drives sales. While the industry has evolved, with a plethora of digital tools and platforms, the age-old art of listening remains paramount.

As we navigate the multifaceted realm of automotive sales, it's essential to remember that our primary role isn't to talk, but to listen. Not just to respond, but to understand. In the simple act of listening, we unlock unparalleled potential — the potential to supercharge sales, foster loyalty, and, above all, truly connect.

As we delve deeper into this book, exploring the nuances of communication, the dynamics of rapport-building, and the intricacies of negotiation, let this first chapter be a foundation stone. An assertion of the undeniable truth that in the orchestra of successful automotive sales, listening isn't just an instrument; it's the very conductor guiding the melody.

Let us harness this power, for in the act of listening, we don't just sell cars; we build bridges, one conversation at a time.

Goals:

1. To understand the foundational importance of listening in effective communication.
2. Recognize how great listeners have an edge in sales and relationship-building.
3. Appreciate how listening affects perception and customer trust.
4. Differentiate between passive and active listening.
5. Embrace the transformative power of truly hearing someone.

Prompts:

1. Recall a time when you felt genuinely listened to. How did that make you feel?
2. Have you ever missed a sales opportunity due to inadequate listening?
3. How do you feel when you realize someone isn't listening to you?

4. What current listening habits might be hampering your sales technique?
5. How can mastering the art of listening change your career trajectory?

Reflections:

1. I felt valued when someone genuinely listened to me.
2. My best sales were often the result of taking the time to listen.
3. The more I listen, the more I learn.
4. Customer trust grows exponentially when they feel heard.
5. Great listeners are often the most influential people.

CHAPTER TWO

UNDERSTANDING THE BASICS OF COMMUNICATION

The art of selling cars—or any product, for that matter—is intrinsically linked to the art of communication. Yet, while sales training often emphasizes persuasion techniques, few dive deep into the foundational principles of communication itself. When an automotive salesperson masters these principles, they don't just sell a car; they create an experience, forging a bond of trust with their customers.

1. Communication: A Two-Way Street

Communication isn't a monologue. It's a dialogue. This means that while conveying information is vital, receiving feedback—through active listening—is equally essential.

Grant Cardone once said, "The best salespeople know that their expertise can become their enemy in selling." What did he mean by this? Sometimes, salespeople become so engrossed in showcasing their knowledge that they forget to tune into the customer's needs, desires, and fears. Hence, understanding the basics of communication ensures that expertise enhances the sales process rather than overpowering it.

2. Verbal and Non-Verbal Cues

Words matter, but so does body language. A study showed that up to 93% of communication effectiveness is determined by non-verbal cues. This includes facial expressions, gestures, posture, and tone of voice. In the context of car sales, a genuine smile, open posture, and a warm tone can make customers feel more at ease, facilitating a smoother sales process.

Zig Ziglar, a man of timeless wisdom, once said, "You can have everything in life you want if you will just help enough other people get what they want." While the words are critical, aligning them with sincere body language reinforces trust and sincerity.

3. Clarity and Brevity

Brian Tracy rightly points out, "The key to success is to focus our conscious mind on things we desire, not things we fear." In sales communication, this means focusing on clarity. Rather than overwhelming customers with excessive jargon or specs, prioritize their primary concerns and interests. Customers often come with an array of desires and fears—whether it's budget constraints, safety features, or the car's aesthetics. Addressing these concerns directly and clearly can dispel fears and move the conversation forward.

4. Open-ended Questions Foster Open Conversations

Open-ended questions—those that can't be answered with a simple 'yes' or 'no'—invite customers to share more about their needs and desires. Questions like, "What are you looking for in your next car?" or "How do you envision using your new vehicle?" prompt the customer to share more, giving the salesperson richer insights.

Grant Cardone notes, "Success is your duty, obligation, and responsibility." As salespeople, it's not just about making the sale but about fulfilling a duty to understand and serve the customer's best interests.

5. Emotional Intelligence: The X-Factor in Communication

While IQ might get someone the technical knowledge about cars, EQ (Emotional Intelligence) will likely get them the sale. EQ is the ability to understand, use, and manage our emotions in positive ways. For salespeople, this translates to recognizing emotions—both theirs and the customer's—and using this awareness to guide their communication strategy.

In today's marketplace, savvy consumers can easily compare features, prices, and reviews. They come into a showroom often equipped with data. So, why do they not just buy online? Why step into a dealership? The answer: emotion. They are looking for an experience, a feeling, something beyond mere specs and numbers. This is where Emotional Intelligence (EQ) becomes invaluable.

Zig Ziglar succinctly said, "People don't buy for logical reasons. They buy for emotional reasons." And if there's one realm where this rings true, it's in the automotive industry. Cars aren't just transportation; they're freedom, they're status, they're milestones, and sometimes, they're even memories.

Let's examine how EQ plays out in practice:

a. Recognizing Emotional Triggers: Imagine a couple walks into the showroom. Through conversation, a salesperson deduces they're expecting their first child. Instead of immediately discussing car sizes or safety features (logic), the salesperson could tap into the emotions of this life-changing event. "Congratulations on the new addition! Having a child is a beautiful journey. Are you looking for a car that ensures safety for your new family member and has room for all those baby essentials?"

b. Sharing Personal Stories: Building on the example above, imagine if the salesperson had recently had a child or has close family who did. Sharing a personal story, "When my sister had her first child, she realized how crucial trunk space was for the stroller, diaper bag, and all those unexpected extras. It's amazing how much a little one can need." This kind of sharing humanizes the salesperson and strengthens the emotional bond with the customer.

c. Mirroring Emotions: If a customer enters the showroom visibly excited, match that enthusiasm. If they seem apprehensive, adopt a more empathetic and calming tone. By mirroring the emotional state of the customer, a salesperson can better align themselves with the customer's journey, making the buying process feel more collaborative.

Real-life example: During my tenure as a general sales manager, I encountered a myriad of customers, each with their unique stories. I distinctly recall one afternoon when a young lady walked into our dealership. She seemed uncertain, frequently glancing at our range of compact cars but not approaching any particular model. Sensing her hesitation, I approached her with a simple, "How can I assist you today?"

She began by stating she was a recent college graduate and was looking for her first car. Instead of launching into a spiel about horsepower, gas mileage, or warranties, I took a different route. "Congratulations on graduating! It must feel like the beginning of a brand new adventure. How does it feel?"

She lit up, sharing her dreams of starting her new job and the independence she craved. As our conversation deepened, it became clear she wasn't just shopping for transportation to get from point A to B. She wanted a symbol of her hard-earned achievement and a partner for the road ahead.

With that insight, I guided her toward a model that not only met her technical needs but also resonated with her emotionally. I shared stories of others who'd been at similar crossroads in their lives, seeking not just a car but a companion for their new journey. By the end of our interaction, she didn't just leave with a car; she left with a story, a symbol of her new beginning. It was not the car's specifications that sealed the deal but the emotional resonance, the promise of adventure, and the embodiment of her newfound independence.

d. Asking Emotionally Driven Questions: Instead of just inquiring about car type preferences, delve deeper. Questions like "What would your dream driving experience feel like?" or "How do you want to feel when you're on the road?" can unlock emotional motivations behind the purchase. When a salesperson taps into EQ, they can seamlessly transition from selling a product to fulfilling a dream, addressing an insecurity, or commemorating a milestone. In doing so, they don't just close a sale; they create a lasting memory associated with that purchase.

6. Adaptability: Pivoting as Per the Customer's Pulse

No two customers are the same. While one might appreciate a detailed rundown of a car's features, another might just want a broad overview followed by a test drive. Being adaptable means sensing the customer's preferences and adjusting the communication style accordingly.

Brian Tracy illuminates this idea further, suggesting, "Approach each customer with the idea of helping him or her solve a problem or achieve a goal, not of selling a product or service." This perspective shift—from selling to assisting—requires adaptability, ensuring that each customer feels uniquely attended to.

7. Building Rapport: The Silent Foundation

In any sales industry, rapport is the bridge that fosters trust between the salesperson and the customer. But in the world of automotive sales, where purchase decisions are significant and often emotionally charged, building rapport isn't just beneficial—it's imperative.

Michael Brooks, author of the book *Building Rapport* writes, "The best salespeople are able to build rapport quickly and easily. They know how to put people at ease and make them feel comfortable talking to them. This is a critical skill, because if you can't build rapport, you won't be able to sell anything."

a. Active Listening: As highlighted in our first chapter, the power of listening is immeasurable. When customers feel heard, they feel valued. So, when a customer talks about wanting a car for weekend family trips, don't just show them the latest model. Discuss the spacious trunk space perfect for camping gear or the entertainment system that will keep kids occupied on long drives.

b. Mirroring and Matching: This is a subtle technique where the salesperson mimics the customer's tone, pace, and even body language. If the customer speaks slowly and deliberately, adapt your speed to match theirs. It creates a subconscious bond and makes interactions more harmonious.

c. Sharing Personal Stories: When appropriate, share a personal story that's related to the customer's situation. If they're looking for a car because they have a new baby on the way, and you've been through that, share it. This not only humanizes you but also makes the customer feel less alone in their journey.

d. Be Genuine: Customers can sense insincerity from a mile away. Avoid being overly agreeable or excessively complimentary. Instead, be genuine in your interactions. If they express concerns about a particular car model based on prior experiences, empathize with their viewpoint and then provide honest feedback or alternative suggestions.

e. Show Consistency: From the initial greeting to post-sale services, maintaining a consistent attitude and behavior is key. It assures the customer that your interest in their well-being wasn't just a sales tactic.

f. Educate, Don't Overwhelm: Often, customers might be unaware of the technicalities of a car. While it's essential to provide information, it's equally important to gauge their comfort level with such details. If they're new to the world of automobiles, break down the jargon. Explain features in a way that pertains to their daily life. For instance, instead of delving deep into the mechanics of an anti-lock braking system, you could simply explain its role in ensuring safer braking during emergencies.

g. Validate Their Concerns: If a customer hesitates over a particular aspect of the purchase, don't brush it aside. Address it head-on. Let's say they're concerned about the resale value of a car. Discuss the brand's reputation in the market, its historical performance, and perhaps even bring in customer testimonials. Recall Cardone's approach of solving problems and achieving goals. Your role as an automotive salesperson extends beyond merely facilitating a purchase. It's about understanding the stories, emotions, and aspirations behind each sale. By building rapport, you're not just selling cars; you're fostering relationships, and these relationships often lead to repeat business, referrals, and a reputation that can set you apart in the industry.

Conclusion

Mastering the basics of communication transcends the act of merely selling cars. It's about connecting, understanding, and fostering relationships. As automotive salespeople embark on this journey of refining their communication skills, they'll find that they aren't just closing more deals—they're enriching their professional relationships, one conversation at a time.

Goals:

1. Grasp the components of effective communication.
2. Comprehend the flow of information from sender to receiver.
3. Recognize barriers to effective communication.
4. Understand non-verbal cues and their significance.
5. Use feedback as a tool to ensure the message was received as intended.

Prompts:

1. What components form the backbone of your communication process?
2. Recall an instance when a miscommunication happened. What went wrong?
3. How often do you consider non-verbal cues in a conversation?
4. Think about a time when feedback changed the direction of a conversation.
5. What barriers do you commonly encounter in communication?

Reflections:

1. Communication is much more than just talking.
2. Body language often conveys more than words.
3. Feedback can be the bridge between confusion and clarity.
4. Every miscommunication offers a lesson to refine my skills.
5. Effective communication is a two-way street.

CHAPTER THREE

THE ART OF ACTIVE LISTENING

For automotive salespeople, the ability to effectively listen plays a pivotal role in sealing the deal. However, the essence of listening isn't just about receiving sound waves; it's about interpreting and understanding the core messages and emotions conveyed by customers. It's this deep comprehension, this art of active listening, that has the potential to transform your sales career.

What is Active Listening?

Active listening is a conscious, focused effort to understand and interpret the speaker's message fully. This is distinctly different from passive listening, where the listener might hear the words but not fully grasp the depth or importance of what's being communicated. It's a dynamic process involving attention, interpretation, and feedback. Active listening in the sales environment, especially within the automotive industry, paves the way for a nuanced understanding of the customer's unique requirements, desires, and concerns.

The Importance of Eliminating Distractions

Let's take an illustrative scenario that emphasizes the value of undivided attention. Imagine a scenario where you're attending an essential training session on the latest car model's features. Eager to learn, you sit ready with your notebook. But every few minutes, the trainer stops to check their phone, leaving you hanging mid-sentence. This repetitive interruption disrupts the flow of information, making it harder for you to understand the full spectrum of features. How would you feel? Likely frustrated and undervalued.

Similarly, every time an automotive salesperson diverts their attention from a customer by taking a phone call or responding to a text, they risk sending an unspoken message: "You're not my top priority right now." Such actions, albeit unintentional, can erode the foundation of trust and mutual respect.

The Power of Presence

Being truly present during interactions with customers goes a long way in the world of sales. A salesperson's genuine presence indicates that they are wholly involved in the conversation, deeply interested in the customer's concerns, and actively seeking to understand their needs. This commitment not only creates a bond of trust but also provides invaluable insights that can be leveraged to tailor your sales pitch perfectly.

Techniques to Enhance Active Listening

1. **Feedback Mechanism:** Summarizing or paraphrasing what the customer has said ensures clarity and reaffirms to the customer that you're engaged.
2. **Non-verbal cues:** Using body language effectively, like maintaining eye contact and nodding occasionally, can communicate your interest without words. It's essential to keep a check on your posture and facial expressions to ensure they align with your intent of being attentive.
3. **Questioning:** Probing with open-ended questions allows you to delve deeper into the customer's thoughts. Instead

of merely asking, "Do you prefer this color?" delve deeper: "How do you feel this color reflects your personality?"

4. **Avoiding Interruptions**: This is pivotal. Give your customers the floor to express themselves fully before you respond. Patience can glean more information than pressure.

5. **Empathy:** This isn't just about feeling but understanding. It's about placing yourself in the customer's position to grasp their emotions, concerns, and aspirations related to the purchase.

The Intersection of Active Listening and Sales Success

Within the automotive industry, nuances can make or break a sale. Perhaps a customer is looking for a vehicle that resonates with their newly acquired status in a job. Another might be searching for a safe and reliable vehicle for their newly licensed teenager. By actively listening, salespeople can identify these nuances and subtly steer the conversation towards vehicles that align perfectly with the customer's narrative.

For instance, if a customer emphasizes safety because they've had a past incident, an active listener would hone in on this and highlight vehicles known for their safety features and ratings.

Moreover, active listening establishes a rapport that goes beyond a mere sales transaction. Customers are more inclined to recommend a salesperson who made them feel understood and valued. In an age where referrals and online reviews can significantly impact business, this cannot be understated.

"You don't close a sale, you open a relationship if you want to build a long-term, successful enterprise." — Patricia Fripp.

The Active Listener's Toolkit

Every automotive salesperson can benefit from refining their active listening toolkit. Here are a few tools to consider:

1. A Journal: Document insights from each interaction. Over time, you'll identify patterns that can guide your sales strategy.
2. A Receptive Mindset: Approach each interaction with genuine curiosity to learn about the customer's world.
3. Feedback Systems: Regularly seek feedback from peers or mentors to identify areas of improvement in your listening skills.
4. Continual Learning: Familiarize yourself with psychological and communication-oriented literature to understand the dynamics of human interaction better.

"If you aim at nothing, you will hit it every time." — Zig Ziglar.

Conclusion

Active listening, in essence, is a commitment—a commitment to understanding, to valuing, and to serving your customer's best interests. In the realm of automotive sales, where each sale is much more than a transaction, it's a relationship; the art of active listening can indeed be a game-changer. By fostering an environment where customers feel genuinely heard and understood, salespeople not only increase their chances of closing a sale but also of opening the door to lasting relationships and continued business.

Goals:

1. Recognize the importance of active engagement during listening.

2. Differentiate between simply hearing and active listening.
3. Understand techniques to stay present during a conversation.
4. Refrain from interrupting and practice patience.
5. Use non-verbal cues to indicate active listening.

Prompts:

1. How often do you find your mind wandering when someone else is talking?
2. What techniques help you stay engaged in a conversation?
3. How do you feel when someone interrupts you mid-conversation?
4. What non-verbal cues do you use to show you're listening?
5. How can you further develop your active listening skills?

Reflections:

1. Active listening requires more effort than I initially thought.
2. Staying present is a continuous challenge but essential for genuine communication.
3. I must strive to listen more than I speak.
4. The more actively I listen, the more I understand my customer's needs.
5. Interruptions can sever the trust bridge I'm trying to build

CHAPTER FOUR

BUILDING RAPPORT THROUGH

LISTENING

In the ever-evolving world of sales, strategies and techniques come and go, but one constant remains evergreen - the power of rapport. In the high-stakes domain of automotive sales, building rapport isn't just a nice-to-have; it's essential. It's a potent bridge that connects salespeople to customers, and at its heart is the art of active listening. This chapter delves deep into how the simple act of listening can be transformative, helping automotive salespeople establish strong connections, earn trust, and ultimately boost sales.

The Essence of Rapport

Rapport is a term often tossed around in sales, sometimes reduced to mere friendly interaction or shared humor.

However, genuine rapport is far deeper and more valuable than a fleeting camaraderie. It's the harmonious connection between two individuals, marked by mutual understanding, trust, and a shared sense of purpose. Building genuine rapport involves more than surface-level pleasantries; it demands sincere interest in the other person, an intention to understand their needs and emotions, and a commitment to aligning with their objectives. When rapport is established, both parties implicitly acknowledge that they're on the same team, working towards a mutual goal.

Why is Rapport Essential in Sales?

1. **Trust Establishment:** People are more inclined to buy from someone they trust. Building rapport fosters trust, laying the foundation for open and honest communication.
2. **Navigating Complex Conversations:** Sales discussions often involve addressing objections, handling concerns, or navigating uncertainties. With strong rapport, these conversations become collaborative problem-solving sessions rather than confrontations.
3. **Long-Term Relationship Building**: While a single sale is valuable, the real gold lies in repeat business and referrals. Rapport paves the way for lasting relationships, transforming one-time buyers into loyal clients.

How to Cultivate Genuine Rapport

Active Listening: Listen intently to your client's words, paying attention to the emotions and concerns beneath the surface. This shows that you genuinely care about their needs and are not solely focused on making a sale.

1. **Find Common Ground:** Discover shared interests or experiences, whether it's a mutual love for a sport, a shared hometown, or similar challenges faced in business.

2. **Be Authentic:** People can spot insincerity from a mile away. Be genuine in your interactions. It's okay to be vulnerable and share a bit about yourself; it humanizes the conversation and builds trust.
3. **Follow Up:** After a sale or even just a conversation, check in with the client. It shows you value the relationship beyond the transaction.

Rapport isn't a sales tactic—it's a way of building genuine connections. It transforms the conventional seller-buyer dynamic into a partnership where both parties are equally invested in a successful outcome. In the vast landscape of sales, where products can be duplicated, and prices can be matched, the ability to build rapport offers a unique and invaluable edge.

Listening: The Key to Unlocking Rapport

Listening is often perceived as a passive act, a mere pause between speaking. However, when done with intent, it becomes one of the most powerful tools in any interpersonal interaction, especially in sales. True listening goes beyond merely hearing words; it's about understanding the emotions, motivations, and needs that drive those words, ultimately unlocking the door to rapport.

Understanding the Power of Listening

1. **Revealing Insights:** When you truly listen to a client, you often discover underlying needs or concerns that may not be explicitly stated. These insights can guide your sales approach, ensuring you address what truly matters to the client.
2. **Demonstrating Respect:** Listening intently signals respect for the speaker. It showcases that their thoughts, feelings, and concerns are valid and worth your time and attention.

3. **Reducing Misunderstandings:** Active listening minimizes the chance of miscommunication, ensuring that both you and the client are on the same page.

The Different Levels of Listening

1. **Cosmetic Listening:** This is the most superficial level, where one appears to be listening but is mostly focused on their own thoughts or distractions.
2. **Conversational Listening:** Here, one listens and responds, but often with their own experiences or solutions. The interaction remains somewhat surface-level.
3. **Active Listening:** This involves fully concentrating on the speaker, understanding, responding, and remembering what is being said. It requires effort and intention.
4. **Deep or Empathetic Listening:** The most profound level. Here, you're not just understanding the words or the emotions; you're connecting deeply, almost feeling what the speaker feels.

Cultivating the Habit of Genuine Listening

1. **Mindful Attention:** Be present in the moment. Push aside external distractions and internal monologues to focus entirely on the speaker.
2. **Encourage Sharing:** Use open-ended questions that allow the client to express themselves more fully.
3. **Reflect and Validate**: Occasionally, reflect back what you've heard to ensure clarity. Validating their feelings or concerns without rushing to solve can create a safe space for open communication.
4. **Resist the Urge to Interrupt:** Even if you believe you have the perfect solution or response, allow the client to

finish their thoughts. Interrupting can be perceived as dismissive.

5. **Maintain Eye Contact:** It not only shows you're attentive but also helps in reading non-verbal cues.

Listening, when approached as an active and intentional skill, becomes the bridge to genuine rapport. In the world of sales, where genuine connections can be the difference between a missed opportunity and a successful deal, mastering the art of listening becomes indispensable. It's not just about sealing the deal; it's about forming relationships built on trust and mutual understanding.

From Transactions to Relationships

Sales, at its core, is about building and nurturing relationships. While traditional sales strategies often focus on closing deals and hitting targets, the more enduring and impactful approach lies in transitioning from a transaction-based mindset to a relationship-centric one. This paradigm shift doesn't just improve the immediate sales experience but fosters long-term loyalty and trust.

Understanding the Difference

1. **Transactions:** These are one-time, often impersonal exchanges. The focus is on the product, the price, and the immediate sale. While transactions might lead to short-term gains, they rarely engender long-term loyalty.

2. **Relationships:** This is about the long game. Instead of focusing on an immediate sale, the emphasis is on understanding the client, catering to their needs, and building a bond that goes beyond the product. A sale within a relationship context isn't just an exchange; it's an affirmation of trust.

Why Relationships Matter in Sales

1. **Repeat Business:** Clients who feel understood and valued are more likely to return for future purchases. This not only assures consistent revenue but reduces the cost and effort of acquiring new customers.
2. **Word of Mouth:** Happy clients often become brand ambassadors, sharing their positive experiences with friends and family, which can lead to new business opportunities.
3. **Feedback Loop:** A strong relationship with clients provides a channel for honest feedback. This can be invaluable in refining products, services, or sales strategies.
4. **Reduced Price Sensitivity:** When clients trust you and the value you provide, they're often less sensitive to price changes, focusing more on the value they derive from the product and the relationship.

The Role of Listening in Building Relationships

1. **Unearthing Needs:** With attentive listening, you can discover both the stated and unstated needs of a client, allowing you to tailor your approach and solutions more effectively.
2. **Building Trust:** When clients feel heard, it lays the foundation for trust. Over time, this trust can translate into loyalty and advocacy.
3. **Navigating Concerns**: Attentive listening also means you pick up on hesitations or concerns early on. Addressing these promptly can prevent potential issues down the road.

Steps to Transition from Transactions to Relationships

1. **Be Genuinely Curious**: Adopt a mindset of genuine interest in your clients. Seek to understand them, not just to sell to them.
2. **Active Engagement:** Interact regularly, not just when there's a sale on the horizon. This could be through follow-ups, updates, or simple check-ins.
3. **Prioritize Their Needs:** While sales targets are essential, prioritize the client's needs above all. This long-term view can yield greater dividends.
4. **Practice Empathy:** Go beyond listening. Feel with the client. Understand their aspirations, challenges, and needs on a deeper level.

In the evolving landscape of sales, where clients are seeking more genuine connections and personalized experiences, the shift from transactions to relationships becomes not just desirable but essential. The cornerstone of this transition is listening —deep, genuine, and with intent. By fostering relationships through attentive listening, sales professionals can transform one-time transactions into enduring bonds.

Empathy vs. Sympathy: Navigating Emotional Landscapes in Sales

Building rapport with clients goes beyond simply understanding their words. It extends to deciphering their emotions and responding appropriately. Often in sales, professionals encounter a spectrum of emotions: excitement, apprehension, indecision, or even frustration. Recognizing and navigating these emotions is crucial, and this requires a deep understanding of the concepts of empathy and sympathy.

Defining the Terms

Empathy: It's a powerful, connective emotion. When you empathize, you're feeling with someone. It involves understanding their emotions from their perspective and genuinely sharing in their feelings. In the realm of sales, empathy allows professionals to not just understand but also to feel a customer's pain points, aspirations, or apprehensions. This is beautifully encapsulated in the words of Dr. Brené Brown, who said, "Empathy fuels connection."

Sympathy: While this, too, is a feeling oriented toward another person's emotional state, it's more detached. Sympathy is feeling for someone. It acknowledges the emotion but doesn't necessarily share in it. While it might sound comforting, it can sometimes come off as dismissive. Dr. Brené Brown adds, "Sympathy drives disconnection."

Why Does It Matter in Sales?

1. **Building Trust**: Empathetic interactions, where the customer feels truly understood, lay a robust foundation for trust. It assures the customer that their concerns or needs are genuinely valued.
2. **Closing Deals:** Customers are more inclined to make purchases when they feel their emotions are recognized and validated. Sympathetic responses might acknowledge their feelings, but without the connection that empathy brings, they might not feel truly heard or understood.
3. **Handling Objections**: With empathy, sales professionals can delve deeper into the root causes of objections or hesitations and address them more effectively.

How to Cultivate Empathy in Sales

1. **Active Listening:** Pay close attention to not just what is being said, but also how it's being conveyed. Notice the emotional undertones.
2. **Avoid Judgment**: Approach every interaction with an open mind. Judging a customer's feelings or needs can hinder genuine empathetic connection.
3. **Ask Open-Ended Questions**: Encourage customers to share more about their feelings. This deepens understanding and can highlight underlying concerns or desires.
4. **Reflect and Validate**: Once you've grasped the customer's emotions, reflect them back in your responses. This validation can be as simple as saying, "I understand why you might feel that way."

Sympathy's Role

While empathy is crucial, sympathy isn't entirely out of place in sales. In situations where you might not have personal experiences to draw from, expressing sympathy—genuine concern and acknowledgment of a customer's feelings—can still provide a bridge of understanding.

In the intricate dance of sales, where every word and gesture can shape outcomes, understanding the nuances between empathy and sympathy becomes paramount. Empathy, as Dr. Brené Brown highlights, truly fuels connection, turning mere interactions into lasting relationships. As sales professionals, striving to empathize with customers' emotional landscapes can pave the way for more genuine connections, deeper trust, and ultimately, success in the sales journey.

The Personal Touch: A Tale from the Showroom Floor

A few years back, a middle-aged man walked in, looking around with a mix of excitement and uncertainty. I greeted him and asked how I could assist him. He mentioned he wanted to buy a car for his daughter's college graduation.

Instead of diving into a sales pitch, I started a conversation. I asked about his daughter, her college, and what she might like in a car. He began to share more details: she was moving to a city for her first job, she loved music, and safety was a big concern for him.

I listened closely and even shared a story about my friend who had a similar experience. This personal touch made him more comfortable. By the time our chat was over, I had a good sense of what he was looking for.

I showed him a few models that would fit his daughter's needs: city-friendly, great sound system, and top safety ratings. He appreciated how I tailored the options based on his story.

In the end, he bought a car that he felt was just right for his daughter. He even sent me a thank you note later, mentioning how happy his daughter was with the gift.

This story shows the value of adding a personal touch in sales. By listening and connecting on a human level, we can better serve our customers. It's not just about selling a product; it's about understanding and meeting the real needs of the person in front of us.

Learning from Legends: The Power of Genuine Listening

When it comes to building strong relationships in sales or any other field, it's always a good idea to learn from those who've been there and done it best. Two giants in the sales arena, Brian Tracy and Grant Cardone, have shared their insights on the importance of listening and rapport. Let's break down their wisdom and see how we can apply it.

Brian Tracy's Take

Brian Tracy once said, "Become a master of listening to your customer and solving his problems." Now, that might sound straightforward, but there's depth to it. What Tracy is telling us is that to truly be successful in sales, we shouldn't just be waiting for our turn to talk. Instead, we need to really hear what the customer is saying. Only by listening can we figure out their problems and offer solutions that fit.

How to Apply Tracy's Wisdom?

1. **Pay Attention:** When a customer talks, give them your full focus. This will help you catch details that might lead to a sale or address a concern.
2. **Ask Clarifying Questions:** If you're unsure about what they're looking for, ask them to explain a bit more. It shows you care about getting it right.

Grant Cardone's Insight

Grant Cardone has shared, "No one is going to buy from you because of your product, company, or compensation plan. They will buy from you because they feel understood." Cardone's point is crystal clear: Sales isn't just about what you're selling; it's about making a connection. If a customer feels like you 'get' them and their needs, they're more likely to trust you and make a purchase.

Applying Cardone's Insight

1. **Build a Connection**: Take a minute to chat with your customer. It doesn't always have to be about the sale. Maybe they mention a recent holiday or a hobby — chat about that.
2. **Reflect Their Needs:** When you discuss your product or service, tailor your pitch to reflect how it addresses their specific needs. Make them feel like you've got just the right solution for them.

Both Tracy and Cardone emphasize the same thing in different ways: the power of listening and understanding. By genuinely listening to your customers and making them feel understood, you're not just selling a product. You're building a relationship, and that's where real sales success lies. In the world of sales, the product or service might be what you're selling, but the connection and trust you build with your customers are what will seal the deal.

Proactive Listening: Turning Simple Hearing into Proactive Listening

While many people believe they're good listeners, there's a significant difference between merely hearing words and truly listening. Listening, especially in sales, goes beyond passive reception of information. It involves an active engagement with what's being said, understanding the underlying messages, emotions, and intentions. This kind of engagement is often termed as proactive listening.

What is Proactive Listening?

Proactive listening is an active form of listening where you're not just absorbing the words spoken but also trying to understand the complete message behind them. This includes understanding the emotions, intentions, and even the unsaid feelings the speaker might be conveying. It's about being fully present in the conversation, making a conscious effort to grasp the full essence of what's being communicated.

The Difference Between Hearing and Listening

Hearing is a passive act. It's a physiological process where sound waves hit our eardrums and get interpreted by our brains. Listening, especially proactive listening, is a conscious choice and requires mental effort. It involves interpreting the information, understanding its significance, and responding to it effectively.

Why is Proactive Listening Crucial in Sales?

1. **Builds Trust:** When customers feel they are genuinely being listened to, they're more likely to trust the salesperson. This trust can be the foundation of a successful sales relationship.
2. **Uncovering Needs:** With attentive listening, a salesperson can detect a customer's real needs, some of which the customer might not even be consciously aware of. This can lead to more effective sales pitches tailored to address those needs.
3. **Avoiding Misunderstandings:** Active engagement reduces the chance of misinterpreting what the customer wants, leading to fewer mistakes and more satisfied customers.

How to Practice Proactive Listening in Sales

1. **Stay Present:** Ensure you're focused entirely on the conversation. Put away distractions, make eye contact, and give your complete attention to the speaker.
2. **Ask Clarifying Questions**: If you're unsure about something, ask. This shows the customer you're genuinely trying to understand their perspective.
3. **Repeat Back:** Every so often, repeat back what you've understood. This not only assures the customer that you're on the same page but also gives them a chance to correct any misunderstandings.
4. **Watch for Non-verbal Cues**: A lot can be said without words. Watch for body language, facial expressions, and tone of voice to get a fuller picture of what's being conveyed.

By adopting proactive listening, salespeople can transform their interactions from mere transactions to meaningful engagements. It's a tool that can elevate the entire sales process, leading to happier customers and better sales outcomes.

Cultivating the Habit of Genuine Interest

The foundation of any deep connection, especially in a sales setting, lies in demonstrating genuine interest. While it's one thing to master the skills of listening, the magic happens when this is combined with a sincere curiosity about the person you're interacting with. This section aims to shed light on the significance of genuine interest and offers insights on how to cultivate this invaluable trait.

The Power of Genuine Interest

When a salesperson showcases true interest in a customer's needs, desires, and concerns, it becomes evident to the customer. This sincerity can lead to:

1. **Building Trust:** Authentic interest fosters trust as customers feel valued and understood.
2. **Deeper Connections:** By showing genuine curiosity, salespeople can dig deeper into the customer's desires and fears, allowing for a more profound connection.
3. **Higher Retention:** Customers are more likely to return to salespeople who showed true interest in their needs, leading to sustained relationships and repeated business.

The Pitfalls of Feigned Interest

While it might be tempting to 'act' interested, customers can often see through insincere gestures. Pretending to be interested can lead to:

1. **Eroded Trust:** If a customer senses they're not genuinely being heard or valued, trust can quickly erode.
2. **Missed Opportunities:** Without genuine interest, a salesperson might miss out on subtle cues or hints from the customer, leading to lost sales opportunities.

Ways to Cultivate Genuine Interest

1. **Practice Active Listening:** As discussed earlier, proactive listening can be a doorway to understanding and resonating with a customer's needs and emotions.
2. **Stay Curious**: Cultivate a mindset of curiosity. Ask open-ended questions and genuinely seek to understand the customer's perspective.
3. **Empathize:** Put yourself in the customer's shoes. Try to understand their emotions, fears, and aspirations.
4. **Continuous Learning:** Invest time in learning about your vehicles, market trends, and potential customer needs. This knowledge will not only boost your confidence but also allow you to engage in more in-depth discussions with customers.

Practical Tips to Demonstrate Genuine Interest

1. **Remember Personal Details:** Simple gestures like recalling a customer's name or referencing a past conversation can go a long way in showing that you truly care.

2. **Follow-up Thoughtfully:** After a sale or even a simple interaction, a thoughtful follow-up can showcase your genuine interest and dedication.
3. **Limit Distractions:** When interacting with a customer, ensure you are fully present. Avoid checking your phone, looking around, or appearing disinterested.

In your market, available inventory and offers might lure customers in, but it's the genuine interest and connection that make them stay. As salespeople aim to build lasting rapport, nurturing a habit of authentic curiosity can be a game-changer, elevating interactions from mere transactions to meaningful relationships.

Conclusion

In the world of automotive sales, where decisions are often significant and impactful, rapport emerges as the silent yet powerful ally of every successful salesperson. By harnessing the power of listening, salespeople can transform standard transactions into meaningful connections, ensuring not just immediate sales but also fostering lasting relationships. As we continue this journey, let the art of listening and the magic of rapport be our guiding lights, leading the way to a future full of meaningful interactions and prosperous outcomes.

Goals:

1. Recognize listening as a key tool in building rapport.
2. Understand the psychological impact of feeling heard.
3. Develop the ability to mirror and match customer's tone and pace.
4. Use listening to identify and tap into the customer's emotional needs.
5. Strengthen customer relationships through genuine engagement.

Prompts:

1. Can you recall a sales scenario where rapport made a significant difference?
2. How do you think listening affects rapport-building?
3. How often do you consciously match a customer's tone or pace?
4. How do you make your customers feel valued during a conversation?
5. What listening techniques have helped you build rapport in the past?

Reflections:

1. Rapport is the silent foundation of a successful sale.
2. People buy from people they like and trust.
3. Every customer wants to feel like they're the only person in the room.
4. Listening actively is one of the highest forms of respect I can give.
5. Genuine engagement often translates to genuine loyalty.

CHAPTER FIVE

EMPATHETIC LISTENING

In the vast spectrum of human interaction, particularly in the automotive sales industry, communication remains the core of every successful transaction. While many focus on the eloquence of their pitches or the persuasion of their words, the true magic lies in how we listen. Enter empathetic listening—a deep, resonant form of listening that transcends mere words, touching the very soul of human emotions. This chapter shines a spotlight on empathetic listening, an approach that can revolutionize automotive sales.

Empathy vs. Sympathy: Delineating the Difference

Navigating the vast seas of human emotions, two terms often arise, seemingly interchangeable but deeply distinct in their essence: empathy and sympathy. To effectively harness the power of empathetic listening, especially in the high-stakes world of sales, one must discern the subtle nuances and profound differences between these two emotions.

The Essence of Empathy:

Empathy is an immersive emotion, a deep dive into the waters of someone else's feelings. It is not just about recognizing another's emotion but genuinely feeling it alongside them. When one empathizes, they temporarily step out of their own world and step into another's, embracing their joys, fears, pains, and hopes as if they were their own. The core of empathy is connection. Dr. Brené Brown, whose work on vulnerability and emotions has inspired many, as stated earlier in this book, "Empathy fuels connection." It's a bridge of understanding that not only acknowledges someone's emotional state but truly resonates with it.

The Essence of Sympathy:

In contrast, sympathy stands on the shoreline, looking out at the vast ocean of someone else's emotions without diving in. It's an acknowledgment from a distance, a form of pity or concern for another's plight without embodying their feelings. Sympathy might recognize another's distress, perhaps even feel sorry for it, but it doesn't connect with the emotion in the profound way empathy does. Again, using Dr. Brown's insightful perspective, "Sympathy drives disconnection." It sends a subtle message of, "I see your pain, but I'm remaining separate from it."

Why the Distinction Matters:

You might wonder, why is distinguishing between empathy and sympathy so pivotal, especially in the realm of sales? The answer lies in the depth of human connection each fosters. Empathy weaves a fabric of deep trust and understanding, laying the foundation for genuine relationships. It says, "I'm with you in this." On the other hand, sympathy, while well-intentioned, often erects a wall, placing the sympathizer and the recipient in separate emotional spaces. In sales, and especially in industries like automotive sales, where emotions run high, such distinctions can be the difference between a successful transaction and a missed opportunity.

Empathy as a Catalyst of Trust:

Consider this: a customer shares a past traumatic experience with cars, and a salesperson responds with, "I'm sorry you went through that" (sympathy). It's a kind acknowledgment, but it might not foster a deep connection. Now, imagine if the salesperson responded with, "That sounds incredibly tough. I can genuinely understand why you'd be cautious moving forward" (empathy). The latter resonates more deeply, fostering an environment of trust and understanding.

The Science Behind Empathetic Listening: A Neurological Perspective

Empathetic listening is not just a feel-good concept or a sales strategy. It's firmly rooted in the intricate mechanisms of the human brain, woven into the very fabric of our neurological systems. When we claim that "empathy is natural," it's not a mere metaphor; it's a scientific fact. To grasp the true potential of empathetic listening, especially in a field as intricate as sales, we must dive deeper into the neurological processes that facilitate empathy.

Mirror Neurons: The Relays of Empathy

One of the most groundbreaking discoveries in the realm of neuroscience in the past few decades has been the identification of mirror neurons. Found in several areas of the brain, these neurons "fire" or activate both when we perform an action and when we observe someone else performing that same action. Essentially, they allow us to "mirror" or simulate others' experiences in our minds.

For instance, when we see someone laugh, not only do the visual areas of our brain light up, but so do the areas associated with our own act of laughing. This mirroring mechanism is believed to be at the heart of empathy. When we engage in empathetic listening, we're not just hearing words; our mirror neurons are actively simulating the emotions conveyed by the speaker, allowing us to "feel" their emotions vicariously.

The Amygdala and Emotional Resonance

The amygdala, a pair of almond-shaped clusters in our brain, plays a pivotal role in emotional processing. It's our emotional radar, always on the lookout for feelings, both in ourselves and others. When engaged in empathetic listening, our amygdala works in tandem with our mirror neurons, discerning emotional cues and ensuring that we don't just understand but also resonate with the feelings of the speaker. This intricate dance between the amygdala and mirror neurons allows us to deeply connect on an emotional level.

The Role of the Prefrontal Cortex

Our ability to empathize is also closely linked to the prefrontal cortex, the brain's executive center. This region helps us regulate our emotions, make decisions, and even predict future outcomes. When we listen empathetically, the prefrontal cortex helps us "tune in" by suppressing our own judgments, biases, and distractions, ensuring a genuine connection with the speaker.

Oxytocin: The Bonding Hormone

Often termed the "love hormone" or "social bonding hormone," oxytocin plays a crucial role in deepening human connections.

Research indicates that elevated oxytocin levels can enhance our ability to empathize with others. Engaging in deep, empathetic listening can stimulate the release of oxytocin, reinforcing the bond between the listener and the speaker.

Empathetic Listening in Action: A Unified Brain

Recent studies using technologies like functional Magnetic Resonance Imaging (fMRI) have shown that when one person is speaking and another is listening empathetically, their brain patterns exhibit remarkable synchronicity. It's as if the listener's brain is "dancing" in harmony with the speaker's, leading to a profound sense of connection.

Empathetic Listening in Automotive Sales: Unleashing Potentials

In the context of automotive sales, empathetic listening unfolds as a transformative strategy. **Here's its potential impact:**

1. **Deepened Connections:** Truly connecting with a customer's emotions, desires, and concerns fosters trust—a key ingredient for any successful sale. This deep-rooted trust streamlines the entire sales process.
2. **Lowered Resistance:** A truly understood customer is a receptive customer. Their defenses wane, skepticism reduces, and they're more open to discussion, making them more amenable to your sales pitch.
3. **Enhanced Solution Tailoring:** By tuning into the emotional frequency of the customer, sales solutions can be better tailored. For example, for a customer anxious about vehicle longevity due to past experiences, a salesperson equipped with empathetic listening might emphasize vehicle reliability and extended warranties.

Navigating the Emotional Terrain: A Step-by-Step Guide

1. **Be Fully Present**: When a customer speaks, immerse yourself. Keep judgments, distractions, or biases at bay.
2. **Decode Nonverbal Cues:** Emotions often resonate more through nonverbal cues. Observing a customer's body language, facial expressions, and tone can provide valuable insights.
3. **Validate Their Emotions**: Once you gauge the customer's emotional state, acknowledge it. Statements like, "That must be tough for you," can bridge emotional gaps.
4. **Ask Open-Ended Questions:** Encourage the customer to delve deeper, expressing more. This not only gives you a clearer picture but also makes the customer feel valued and understood.

Empathetic Listening in Action: A Sales Tale

One day, I was at the car dealership when a young woman walked in. She looked around with interest, but there was a hint of worry in her eyes. I approached her to see if she needed any help, and she mentioned she was looking for her first car. It was clear she was excited but also a bit nervous.

I could have immediately shown her the latest models, but instead, I chose to listen. I asked her what she was looking for in a car. She started talking about how the city's heavy traffic and the challenge of parking in tight spots made her anxious.

Instead of jumping straight to a sales pitch, I listened more and tried to understand her concerns. I nodded and showed her that I got where she was coming from. Once she finished explaining, I thought about cars that would be a good fit for a new driver like her, especially in a busy city.

I showed her a few compact models known for their safety features. I told her about their easy handling and the technology they had to help with parking. I also shared some stories of other first-time drivers who found these models easy to drive and park.

She looked relieved and grateful. By addressing her specific concerns, she felt more confident in making a decision. In the end, she bought a car, not because of some flashy sales pitch but because she felt understood.

This experience taught me the real power of empathetic listening in sales. It wasn't about pushing a product; it was about understanding a person's needs and feelings. By doing so, not only did the sale become easier, but it also became more meaningful.

Conclusion: Embracing Empathy in Informative Sales

In the ever-evolving realm of automotive sales, where emotions, aspirations, and dreams intertwine with every transaction, empathetic listening stands tall as an invaluable asset. By genuinely resonating with the emotions of customers, sales representatives can build lasting relationships, craft impeccable solutions, and elevate their sales performance. As we navigate this journey, let empathy be our compass, transforming automotive sales into a symphony of genuine human connections.

Goals:

1. Deeply understand the emotions behind the words of the speaker.
2. Differentiate between sympathy and empathy in listening.
3. Use empathetic listening to address customer concerns effectively.
4. Build stronger emotional connections with customers.
5. Enhance trust and understanding through empathy.

Prompts:

1. Think of a time when someone showed genuine empathy towards you. How did it feel?
2. How can empathetic listening change the dynamics of a sales conversation?
3. How do you handle a customer's emotions during a sale?
4. Can you recall a situation where empathy helped in resolving a customer's concern?
5. How often do you find yourself sympathizing rather than empathizing?

Reflections:

1. Empathy often feels like a balm on an emotional wound.
2. Understanding emotions can pave the path to solving real concerns.
3. Every customer has a story; it's my job to listen to it.
4. Trust is built when customers feel genuinely understood.
5. Empathy is not just hearing; it's feeling with the customer.

CHAPTER SIX

UNCOVERING CUSTOMER NEEDS

The ability to uncover and address customer needs is crucial for successful selling. Learn to ask probing questions and effectively uncover their needs. By mastering the art of uncovering customer needs through empathetic listening, you can tailor your solutions and create more meaningful connections.

Active listening is the foundation for uncovering customer needs. It involves giving your full attention to the customer's words, focusing on understanding their challenges, goals, and desires. By listening attentively, you can identify valuable cues and insights that guide your sales approach.

Probing questions are powerful tools for eliciting deeper insights into customer needs. These open-ended questions encourage customers to provide more detailed responses, allowing you to gain a thorough understanding of their pain points and aspirations. By asking questions such as "Can you tell me more about that?" or "If the price were the same, which vehicle would you choose and why?" you invite customers to share more information and provide you with a clearer picture of their needs.

Uncovering the true needs of a customer is the cornerstone of successful sales. Often, the hesitation to delve deep and probe can be the biggest roadblock for salespeople, especially in the automotive industry. But, just like any competent professional, salespeople must navigate beyond superficial exchanges to provide real value.

The Fear of Probing Deep:

Asking questions, especially ones that push beyond surface-level interactions, can be a daunting task for many salespeople. The fear of probing deep arises from:

- Fear of Being Intrusive: The trepidation that the customer may perceive probing questions as invasive or prying, risking the rapport built.
- Assumptions and Predictions: Believing that the initial interactions or basic details are enough to gauge what the customer desires.
- Staying in the Comfort Zone: Keeping interactions light and superficial is often seen as the safer route, avoiding potential confrontations or difficult situations.

By side-stepping the essential questions, salespeople might miss out on critical information about the customer's true needs, leading to missed opportunities. To address this, Daniel H. Pink aptly notes in his book *Drive*, "Human beings have an innate inner drive to be autonomous, self-determined, and connected to one another. And when that drive is liberated, people achieve more and live richer lives." To be connected with a customer, a salesperson must be brave enough to ask, to probe, and to understand.

Seeing Beyond the Obvious: The Doctor-Patient Paradigm:

One of the most illustrative examples of the importance of deep probing is seen in the medical profession. A patient's initial complaints or self-diagnosis is merely the tip of the iceberg. A competent doctor looks beyond, asks questions, and deduces the underlying problem. Similarly, for a salesperson, the initial inquiry or expression of interest from a customer is just the beginning.

Imagine, if you will, a patient entering a clinic with a persistent headache. They've self-diagnosed it as a result of stress. Without further probing, a doctor might prescribe painkillers. However, deeper questions might reveal the headache is due to eyesight issues, and what the patient really needs are glasses, not painkillers.

This analogy is a clarion call for salespeople to see their role as consultants. Understanding that the first solution that pops up might not be the best, and sometimes, the customer isn't even aware of what they truly need.

As Simon Sinek insightfully remarks in *Start With Why*, "People don't buy WHAT you do; they buy WHY you do it." The true "why" is hidden in the deeper layers of conversation and can only be revealed through profound questioning.

Strategies to Unearth the Concealed Needs:

Uncovering the hidden treasures of customer needs requires a strategic approach:

1. **Foster Trust:** Begin by creating a foundation of trust. Exhibit genuine concern, warmth, and authenticity. Ensure the customer feels valued and understood.

2. **The Power of Empathy:** Being empathetic creates a deeper connection. *Emotional Intelligence* by Daniel Goleman emphasizes, "Empathy represents the foundation skill for all the social competencies important for work." By viewing the world from the customer's perspective, a salesperson can cater to their real needs.

3. **Ask Open-Ended Questions:** These are gateways to deeper insights. Instead of questions that elicit a mere "yes" or "no," encourage customers to share more by asking who, what, and why.

4. **Change the Mindset:** Rather than viewing questions as potential obstacles or points of discomfort, see them as the bridges to understanding. It's through these bridges that genuine solutions can be crafted.

5. **Acknowledgment is Key:** As the customer shares, it's vital to acknowledge their feelings and perspectives. Simple nods, reaffirming words, or short statements can make all the difference.

Conclusion: The Power of Probing

Sales is an art. An art that demands understanding, finesse, and genuine care. When salespeople shift from seeing sales as mere transactions to viewing them as relationships, the results can be transformative.

As Mark Goulston aptly states in his book *Just Listen*, "The most powerful form of acknowledgment is simply listening." When salespeople listen with genuine interest and probe to understand better, they not only uncover customer needs but also build lasting relationships.

So, the next time a customer walks into your dealership, view them not as a mere transaction opportunity but as a relationship waiting to be built. Dive deep, ask those vital questions, and provide value that resonates. The sales, satisfaction, and success that follow will be testament to the power of true understanding.

In addition to asking probing questions, it is essential to listen actively for indirect or implicit customer needs. Sometimes, customers may not explicitly state their needs, but they might drop hints or express dissatisfaction in certain areas. By paying attention to these subtle cues and reading between the lines, you can uncover underlying needs that the customer may not have explicitly shared. This ability to listen beyond the surface level allows you to offer tailored solutions that address their unspoken concerns.

Empathy plays a vital role in uncovering customer needs. By empathetically listening to your customers, you can put yourself in their shoes and understand their challenges from their perspective. This deep understanding enables you to identify needs that may not be immediately apparent and provide solutions that genuinely resonate with their experiences. When customers feel heard and understood, they are more likely to trust your recommendations and choose your offerings.

Active listening also involves being attuned to non-verbal cues. While customers may express their needs verbally, their non-verbal communication can reveal additional insights. Pay attention to their body language, facial expressions, and tone of voice, as these cues can indicate underlying emotions or preferences. For example, a customer's excitement or enthusiasm may indicate a specific need or desire that you can address. Find a way to focus on the solution to their needs, not hoping they'll spend more money on what they think they want.

It is important to note that uncovering customer needs through listening is an ongoing process. Needs can evolve over time, and customer preferences may change. Therefore, maintaining open lines of communication and continuously listening to your customers is essential. Regularly check in with them, seek feedback, and stay attuned to any new challenges or aspirations they may have. By staying actively engaged and responsive to their evolving needs, you can foster long-term customer loyalty.

Uncovering customer needs through active listening is a pivotal aspect of successful selling. By listening attentively, asking probing questions, reading between the lines, practicing empathy, and being attuned to non-verbal cues, you can gain a comprehensive understanding of your customers' needs and provide tailored solutions. This approach allows you to create meaningful connections, build trust, and position yourself as a trusted advisor who genuinely listens and addresses their specific needs. By mastering the art of uncovering customer needs through listening, you can create a customer-centric sales approach that drives mutual success and fosters long-lasting relationships.

Goals:

1. Master the art of probing without seeming intrusive.
2. Understand the difference between a want and a need.
3. Use listening as a tool to uncover underlying needs.
4. Position your product or service based on revealed needs.
5. Build sales strategies around genuine customer requirements.

Prompts:

1. How do you differentiate between a customer's stated wants and their actual needs?
2. How has listening helped you uncover a need the customer wasn't even aware of?

3. Can you think of a sale that was successful because you addressed an underlying need?
4. How do you ensure you're not being too intrusive when probing?
5. How often do you tailor your sales approach based on uncovered needs?

Reflections:

1. Every customer conversation is a goldmine of information.
2. Addressing real needs leads to satisfied customers and repeat business.
3. The difference between a want and a need can be subtle but crucial.
4. Probing is an art, balancing between curiosity and respect.
5. Tailoring my approach based on customer needs often leads to more fruitful outcomes.

CHAPTER SEVEN

QUESTIONING TECHNIQUES FOR

BETTER LISTENING

Many assume that questioning is just about collecting information or satisfying one's curiosity. However, its impact reaches further than these basic areas. What makes questioning so crucial to effective listening, and why can't we simply let individuals express themselves without interruptions?

The Relationship Between Questions and Psychology

Everyday conversations can be quite surface-level, but the depth and richness of discussions often depend on the kinds of questions posed. As George T. Thompson describes in *Verbal Judo*, "Questions are like keys that open up different reactions, details, and feelings. But you need to use the right key for the right door." Just as specific keys match certain locks, effective questioning helps access specific emotions or details from an individual.

By asking questions, listeners convey their true engagement in the conversation, showing a deep desire to truly understand, not just hear. Questions challenge speakers to think deeper and express more clearly, leading to better dialogues. They also steer the direction of discussions, ensuring clarity and purpose.

For salespeople, if a customer shares a preference and they don't ask further questions, they might make wrong assumptions or end the chat too soon. Digging deeper could reveal essential factors that affect the final decision. No, questions are crucial for both collecting details and building rapport.

Types of Questions: Tools for Listeners

1. **Open-Ended Questions:** Broad queries that seek detailed responses. E.g., "What features do you prioritize in a car?"
2. **Closed-Ended Questions:** Specific queries for short answers. E.g., "Do you prefer manual or automatic?"
3. **Probing Questions:** These go deeper into given answers. If someone says, "I want a roomy car," you might ask, "How many passengers do you usually have?"
4. **Clarifying Questions:** To ensure clear understanding. If someone says, "I don't want a big car," you might ask, "What size or model are you thinking of?"
5. **Reflective Questions:** Reflects what the speaker said for confirmation. E.g., "No, you're looking for a fuel-efficient yet rugged car."
6. **Hypothetical Questions:** Gauge reactions to potential scenarios. "If there was a car that ticked all your boxes but was a bit pricey, would you still consider it?"

High-Stakes Questioning

In a world where communication is pivotal to understanding and decision-making, the significance of questioning magnifies exponentially when the stakes are high. High-stakes scenarios demand precision, accuracy, and tact, where one misstep can have profound consequences.

The Essence of High-Stakes Questioning

High-stakes questioning isn't merely about getting answers; it's about understanding the depth of a situation, gauging emotions, and formulating strategies. Whether it's in international diplomacy, criminal interrogations, or even high-stakes business negotiations, the questions posed determine the direction and outcome of the dialogue.

FBI Interrogations: A Study in Expert Questioning

Let's take the FBI as a prime example. FBI agents, especially hostage negotiators, are trained in the subtle art of questioning to extract crucial information without escalating a volatile situation. Chris Voss, in his book *Never Split the Difference*, shares invaluable insights from his time as an international hostage negotiator for the FBI. Voss elaborates on the concept of "calibrated questions," which are carefully crafted to give the respondent a sense of control, making them more amenable to sharing information. Such questions are less about asserting dominance and more about building a bridge of understanding.

Business Negotiations: High Stakes in the Corporate World

Transitioning from crime scenes to boardrooms, high-stakes questioning plays a pivotal role in business negotiations as well. When millions of dollars are on the line, or a company's future is at stake, the ability to ask the right questions becomes invaluable. It's not just about understanding the other party's position but about unveiling underlying motivations, constraints, and aspirations. Effective questioning can make the difference between a successful merger and a missed opportunity.

Techniques for Effective High-Stakes Questioning

1. **Active Listening:** Before formulating a question, listen intently. Understanding the nuances and undertones can guide the line of inquiry.
2. **Open-Ended Questions:** Such questions allow for expansive answers, offering more insights. Instead of asking, "Do you agree?" one might ask, "How do you feel about this proposal?"
3. **Avoiding Leading Questions:** In high-stakes scenarios, leading questions can come across as manipulative. It's essential to remain neutral.
4. **Empathetic Inquiry:** Show genuine concern and interest. It can be as simple as, "Can you help me understand your perspective on this?"

The Consequences of Inadequate Questioning in High-Stakes Scenarios

It's also essential to recognize the potential fallout of poor questioning. In high-stakes situations, a mis-phrased or ill-timed question can escalate tensions, cause misunderstandings, or even lead to unfavorable outcomes. The weight of responsibility in such scenarios underscores the importance of mastering the art of questioning.

High-stakes questioning is an art that demands a blend of tact, empathy, and strategy. It's a tool that, when wielded correctly, can unravel complex scenarios, bridge understanding gaps, and pave the way for optimal outcomes in tense situations. Whether on the global stage, in a police standoff, or at a corporate negotiation table, effective questioning remains a cornerstone of successful communication.

The Risks of Poor Communication

In the high-stakes world of automotive sales, communication is not just a skill; it's the lifeblood that keeps the sales process alive and thriving. When communication falters in this dynamic environment, the ripples can be felt across the dealership, from the sales floor to the service bay, and even in the customer's driveway. Let's explore the unique risks associated with poor communication specifically in the realm of automotive sales.

Lost Sales and Reduced Commissions

First and foremost, the most immediate repercussion of miscommunication in automotive sales is the potential loss of a sale. A customer's needs, budget constraints, or concerns, if misunderstood or overlooked, can quickly turn an eager prospect into a disenchanted visitor. This not only impacts the dealership's bottom line but directly hits the pockets of the sales professionals in the form of reduced commissions.

Damage to Dealership Reputation

In an age where online reviews can make or break a business, a single instance of poor communication can lead to negative feedback. A customer who feels misunderstood or misled is likely to share their experience online, which can deter potential customers and tarnish the dealership's reputation.

Missed Opportunities for Upselling

Effective communication allows sales professionals to gauge a customer's needs, preferences, and financial capabilities. Miscommunication can result in missed opportunities to upsell additional features, warranties, or service packages that would have added value to the customer and increased the sale's profitability.

Inefficient Inventory Management

Communication isn't just essential with customers; it's crucial internally. Misunderstandings between the sales and inventory teams can lead to inefficient inventory management. If a sales professional is unaware of what's available, they might miss out on promoting vehicles that are overstocked or fail to order a specific model a customer desires.

Post-Sale Service Conflicts

A car sale often doesn't end when the customer drives off the lot. Miscommunication during the sales process about warranties, service inclusions, or maintenance schedules can lead to conflicts when the customer returns for service or repairs. This can strain the relationship between sales and service departments and lead to customer dissatisfaction.

Prolonged Sales Cycles

Without clear communication, the sales process can become drawn out, as misunderstandings need to be clarified and decisions reevaluated. This not only frustrates the customer but also ties up the sales professional, preventing them from engaging with new potential clients.

Decreased Customer Loyalty

Automotive sales are not just about the one-time purchase; it's about building a relationship of trust, ensuring repeat business, and gaining referrals. Poor communication can jeopardize this relationship, making it unlikely for the customer to return for their next purchase or recommend the dealership to friends and family.

Legal Repercussions

In some instances, especially concerning contracts, warranties, and financing, miscommunication can have legal implications. Misleading a customer, whether intentional or due to misunderstanding, can result in lawsuits, adding financial strain and further damaging the dealership's reputation.

For the automotive sales professional, mastering the art of communication is non-negotiable. It's a skill that directly impacts their success, the dealership's reputation, and the satisfaction of their customers. Recognizing the risks of poor communication and proactively refining one's communication techniques can spell the difference between a thriving career in automotive sales and a series of missed opportunities.

Conclusion: Question to Understand, Understand to Succeed

Going through a conversation without questions is like wandering in a dark room. For car salespeople, the goal is not just to chat but to truly understand, connect, and provide solutions. Asking questions illuminates the way, making the sales process more focused and effective.

To excel in automotive sales, one needs more than smooth talk; they must be a smart questioner and an attentive listener. After all, every question asked is a step closer to understanding, trust, and a successful sale.

Goals:

1. Develop a repertoire of open-ended questions.
2. Use questions as tools to steer and deepen conversations.
3. Understand the power of silence in questioning.
4. Encourage customers to share more through effective questioning.
5. Differentiate between probing and leading questions.

Prompts:

1. What are your go-to open-ended questions during a sale?
2. How do you feel when someone uses leading questions on you?
3. Can you think of a time when silence after a question led to a valuable insight?
4. How do you encourage a hesitant customer to open up?
5. What questioning techniques have you found most effective?

Reflections:

1. The quality of my questions often determines the quality of the responses.
2. Silence can be a powerful tool, offering space for deeper revelations.
3. Leading questions can often backfire, making genuine engagement crucial.
4. Every question is an opportunity to understand better and serve more effectively.
5. Listening is as much about asking the right questions as it is about hearing the answers.

CHAPTER EIGHT

LISTENING TO UNDERSTAND, NOT TO RESPOND

In our fast-paced world, many of us often find ourselves preparing our next statement even before the person in front of us finishes their sentence. As Stephen R. Covey astutely noted, "Most people do not listen with the intent to understand; they listen with the intent to reply." In automotive sales, this isn't just an oversight; it can be a critical misstep. Preempting what a client might say or want can lead you to miss out on important information, sentiments, or buying signals.

Rethinking "Always Be Closing:"

The phrase "always be closing" has been drilled into the mind of every salesperson. Its intent is positive, urging salespeople to be proactive in sealing deals. However, in automotive sales, there's a risk. It can steer salespeople into thinking only about quick responses and immediate closes, leading them to miss the nuances of the conversation.

Consider a situation:

A client mentions their love for a solid sound system in a car. While it might be tempting to instantly pitch a model with the latest sound system, that's just scratching the surface. Maybe this client recalls joyful memories of road trips with music as their companion. Without delving deeper, you'll miss the emotion driving their choice.

Empathetic Listening: The Game Changer:

Empathy means connecting with others. Brené Brown, in *Dare to Lead*, captures its essence perfectly, "Empathy is feeling with people." For car salespeople, this means truly understanding a client's story, needs, and concerns. So, instead of pitching right away, maybe ask, "I see you value a good sound system. Any special reason behind that?" This simple tweak makes clients feel valued.

Building Trust through Understanding:

When clients sense you're genuinely trying to understand them, they begin to trust you. As Paul A. Argenti highlights in *Strategic Corporate Communication*, "Trust is the foundation of any relationship, and relationships are the key to successful communication." In the automotive sales landscape, this trust can lead to both immediate sales and long-term loyalty.

Listening to truly understand casts you in the role of a trusted advisor rather than just a salesperson. This deepens relationships and can lead to more referrals and repeat sales.

Steps to Enhance Understanding:

1. **Stay Present:** When a client speaks, be in the moment. Drop any rehearsed answers and really listen.
2. **Look for Non-Verbal Signs**: A client's gestures, facial expressions, and posture can reveal more than words. Is there excitement, doubt, or perhaps some anxiety?
3. **Ask Open Questions**: Avoid questions that elicit a mere 'yes' or 'no.' "How do you see this car fitting into your daily life?" can yield more insight than you'd expect.
4. **Reiterate**: Reflecting back what the client said can ensure you're on the same page and shows them you're truly engaged.
5. **Avoid Cutting Off:** Let the client finish. It's basic courtesy and can give you more information.

The Power of Real Listening:

In the bustling world of automotive sales, there's often a race to show, tell, and sell. Amidst the clamor of features, models, and deals, the subtle power of real listening can get overlooked. However, for those in the know, genuine listening isn't just a passive act—it's the bedrock of effective sales.

When we think of listening, we often visualize it as merely hearing the words spoken to us. But real listening goes far beyond that. It's about diving deep into the underlying emotions, intentions, and desires that fuel those words. When a customer talks about the importance of safety in a car, they're not just referring to features. They might be echoing concerns for their family, memories of past incidents, or aspirations for secure journeys ahead. Recognizing and acknowledging this depth can change the entire dynamics of a sales conversation.

Real listening is like having a magnifying glass that can highlight the hidden desires and concerns of customers. For instance, a young parent might drop subtle hints about the importance of space for baby gear, or a college graduate might imply the need for an affordable yet stylish car model. By tuning into these cues, a salesperson can tailor their pitch to resonate with the customer's actual needs.

It's no secret that trust is a vital ingredient in the sales recipe. However, trust isn't something that can be forced or fast-tracked with flashy presentations. It grows over time, and one of its primary nutrients is genuine listening. When customers feel heard, when they see that their words and emotions matter, they're more inclined to trust the person on the other side of the conversation.

In the sales arena, objections are a common occurrence. However, the power of real listening provides salespeople with an intuitive edge to navigate these challenges. By truly understanding the root of a customer's hesitation or concern, a salesperson can address it with pinpoint accuracy, instead of offering generic solutions.

The automotive industry isn't just about one-time sales; it's about building long-lasting relationships. A client who feels understood today becomes a brand ambassador tomorrow. They're more likely to return for future purchases, recommend the dealership to friends and family, and even provide invaluable feedback. All of this starts with the simple yet powerful act of real listening.

While skills, product knowledge, and sales strategies are crucial, the power of real listening stands out as an unsung hero in the automotive sales domain. It's an investment that requires patience, empathy, and genuine interest, but its returns, in the form of satisfied customers and robust sales figures, are undeniable. In a world filled with noise, taking a moment to truly listen can set you apart and propel your sales journey to unparalleled heights.

The Ripple Effect of Genuine Listening:

While making that sale is the immediate goal, true understanding has benefits that ripple far beyond the showroom floor. A client who feels understood today is more likely to return tomorrow, not just for another purchase but also for other services you offer. Moreover, the bond of trust and understanding you establish makes you the first name they recommend when a friend or family member is in the market for a new vehicle.

The role of an automotive salesperson is evolving. It's no longer just about showcasing car features or the best finance options. It's about understanding the lifestyle, needs, and emotions of the potential buyer. It's about being a consultant who can recommend the best fit. And this evolution is being fueled by the power of genuine listening.

Remember, each client walking into your showroom has a unique story. While one might be looking for a family car to ensure safety for their children, another might want a vehicle that's a status symbol. By actively listening, you can tailor your approach, ensuring that you're addressing their specific desires and concerns.

An often-overlooked benefit of genuine listening is the cultivation of repeat business. When clients feel they're truly being heard, they're more likely to come back, whether it's for a service, a new purchase, or even to share their positive experience with friends and family.

Another advantage of active listening is feedback. Customers often provide valuable insights about what they like or dislike, which can be relayed back to manufacturers or used to improve the overall buying experience. This continuous feedback loop, facilitated by genuine listening, ensures that you're always ahead of the curve.

Conclusion:

The art of true listening is transformative. In the high-octane world of automotive sales, where decisions are made swiftly, taking a moment to genuinely listen can make all the difference. It's not merely about sealing today's deal but about creating a legacy of trust, loyalty, and mutual respect that ensures success for years to come.

Goals:

1. Cultivate patience and resist the urge to formulate responses prematurely.
2. Understand the pitfalls of the "always be closing" mindset.
3. Prioritize understanding over immediate rebuttal.
4. Use listening as a tool to truly comprehend customer perspectives.
5. Enhance customer trust by showing genuine understanding.

Prompts:

1. How often do you find yourself formulating responses before the customer finishes speaking?
2. Can you recall a time when waiting to respond led to a better outcome?

3. How has the "always be closing" mindset affected your sales in the past?
4. What techniques help you focus more on understanding than on responding?
5. How do you feel when you realize someone is only waiting for their turn to speak?

Reflections:

1. Genuine understanding is the bedrock of trust.
2. Taking the time to understand can change the trajectory of a sale.
3. Immediate responses can sometimes be immediate missteps.
4. Every customer wants to be understood, not just heard.
5. Waiting before responding often leads to more insightful interactions.

CHAPTER NINE

THE ROLE OF LISTENING IN NEGOTIATION

At the heart of every successful negotiation, especially in the competitive world of automotive sales, is the often-underestimated act of listening. As we delve into the labyrinth of negotiation strategies, we realize that it isn't about aggressively pushing a point, but instead understanding the other side. Dean Rusk, the former U.S. Secretary of State, puts it simply yet powerfully: "One of the best ways to persuade others is by listening to them."

Decoding the Essence of Negotiation

In the demanding and ever-evolving sphere of car sales, grasping the true essence of negotiation is paramount. Each engagement with a potential buyer is a nuanced exchange of words, gestures, and intentions. Both the salesperson and the customer enter this dialogue with distinct goals and aspirations. However, what often distinguishes successful salespeople from the rest isn't just their in-depth product knowledge or polished sales tactics, but their proficiency in the art of listening.

Discussing negotiation in car sales goes beyond mere haggling over prices or pushing for added perks. At its core, negotiation revolves around understanding. Every customer stepping into the showroom brings with them a narrative, a set of past experiences, and specific desires and concerns. They aren't merely in search of a vehicle; they are in pursuit of a solution, an experience, a fit for their unique requirements.

Imagine two sales scenarios. In the first, a salesperson quickly offers discounts or begins describing the newest features as soon as the customer raises a concern about price or value. In the second scenario, the salesperson pauses, listens keenly, absorbing not just the spoken words but the emotions that accompany them. This salesperson seeks to decipher the 'why' before delving into the 'what.' Why is this particular customer concerned about the price? Is it due to a tight budget, a previous regrettable purchase, or perhaps a gap in understanding the car's distinctive features?

Roger Fisher's influential work *Getting to Yes* underscores that the crux of successful negotiation is rooted in understanding, especially in distinguishing the individual from the challenge at hand. Within the realm of car sales, this means looking beyond the immediate transaction to truly understand the person you're engaging with. It's about recognizing that the young couple isn't merely seeking a spacious car; they're anticipating a family. The retiree isn't just downsizing; they might be hunting for a vehicle that's simpler to handle and maintain.

Empathetic listening becomes the catalyst for this profound understanding. It's an active endeavor, demanding the salesperson to be fully present, to pick up on the subtle cues - a hesitant voice, a spark of excitement in the eyes, or a fleeting look of uncertainty. It involves posing open-ended questions, allowing the customer to express freely, and reflecting back to ensure clarity and display genuine interest.

In the realm of automotive sales, where every conversation holds potential, deciphering the essence of negotiation through empathetic listening emerges as a pivotal skill. It elevates a typical sales interaction into a memorable buying journey, paving the way not just for immediate sales but for fostering enduring customer relationships.

Climbing the Listening Ladder

1. **Surface-Level Listening:** The starting point where the negotiator simply catches words without genuinely processing them, often being preoccupied with their next move.
2. **Active Listening:** A step up, where one genuinely tries to get the gist of what's being conveyed, possibly by nodding in agreement or seeking clarification.
3. **Empathetic Listening:** The zenith of listening in negotiation. Here, the aim is to grasp the feelings and reasons behind the spoken words, building a true bridge of trust.

William Ury, a negotiation genius and co-author of *Getting to Yes*, emphasizes that true trust in negotiations is birthed from empathetic listening. It's more than just a skill; it's a philosophy.

Understanding the Customer Through Empathetic Listening

Imagine this: you're at your dealership, and your customer is set on a specific price. You might just think, "Oh, they're trying to bargain," and stop at that. But if you're an empathetic listener, you think differently. You ask yourself why. Why is this customer stuck on this price?

Empathetic listening is like having a tool that lets you see more than what's right in front of you. It's like putting on special glasses that show you things others might miss. So, when a customer is firm on a price, these glasses help you see the reasons behind it.

Could it be that they have a tight budget? We all know how tough times can be, and maybe they have a limit on what they can spend. Or perhaps, in the past, they bought a car and later felt like they paid too much. No one likes that feeling of regret. Or it might be simpler; maybe they just don't see why the car should cost more than the price they have in mind.

Chris Voss, who wrote "Never Split the Difference," talks about something called tactical empathy. This is a fancy term, but it's actually quite simple. It means understanding how the other person feels and then using that understanding to have a good conversation. Think about it like this: if you know why someone feels a certain way, you can talk to them in a way that makes sense to them.

In car sales, this is super important. Every customer is different. They come from different places, have different stories, and want different things. By listening carefully and trying to understand where they're coming from, you can talk to them in a way that meets their needs. And when customers feel understood, they are more likely to trust you.

So, the next time a customer comes in with a firm price in mind or any other specific request, try to use empathetic listening. Listen closely, think about why they might feel that way, and then use that understanding to guide your conversation. It's a simple way to make your job easier and make your customers happier.

Sealing the Deal with Feedback

True listening is a two-way street. In the realm of car sales, once you've genuinely listened, it's vital to echo back what you've understood. For instance, a phrase like, "You seem to really prioritize fuel efficiency. Is that due to a lot of daily commuting?" can be a game-changer, reaffirming to the customer that they are truly being heard.

Moving from Competition to Cooperation

The traditional view of negotiations can often feel like a boxing match, with each side trying to out-punch the other. Every move is calculated to gain an upper hand. But if we look at modern sales dynamics, especially in the automotive sector, it's clear that this approach is becoming outdated.

Deepak Malhotra, in *Negotiating the Impossible*, brings forward a refreshing take. Instead of seeing the negotiation table as a battlefield, he encourages us to view it as a meeting of minds, a place where mutual solutions are crafted. In essence, it's moving from a mindset of "I win, you lose" to "let's both win."

In the automotive industry, customers come with more than just a need for a vehicle; they come with experiences, expectations, and emotions. The success of a sale often hinges on the salesperson's ability to tap into these factors, understand them, and navigate the negotiation waters with this understanding in tow.

When you're selling cars, it's not just about that one sale. It's about building a relationship that could lead to more sales in the future, either through repeat business or referrals. If a negotiation feels combative, even if the sale is secured, the customer may walk away with a negative experience. They might buy the car but never return for a future purchase or, worse, share their negative experience with others.

Collaborative negotiations, on the other hand, leave both parties feeling satisfied. They've been part of a process where their needs were heard, understood, and met as closely as possible.

Here's where empathetic listening becomes crucial. Let's look at a different scenario: A customer walks into the dealership and immediately gravitates toward the pre-owned section. They seem hesitant about approaching the latest models. Rather than pushing the new arrivals, which could yield a higher commission, a salesperson adopting a collaborative approach might start a conversation to understand this preference.

By listening, they might discover that the customer has concerns about depreciation or has always bought pre-owned because they believe they're getting a better deal. With this understanding, the salesperson can then present the benefits of the newer models, maybe discussing warranties, advanced safety features, or better fuel efficiency. The conversation is no longer about just making a sale, but about addressing specific customer concerns, ensuring they make an informed decision.

Genuine listening builds trust. In car sales, trust can be the difference between a one-time buyer and a loyal customer. When customers feel that their concerns are being addressed, and they're not just being "sold to," they're more likely to engage positively.

Implementing Collaboration in Everyday Negotiations

To make collaboration an integral part of your negotiation strategy:

1. **Start with Open-ended Questions:** Allow the customer to share their story, their concerns, and their needs.
2. **Practice Active Listening:** When a customer speaks, give them your full attention. Avoid interrupting or formulating your response while they're still talking.
3. **Aim for Mutual Benefits:** Find solutions where both you and the customer gain something valuable.
4. **Prioritize Relationships:** See every negotiation not as a one-off deal but as a step in building a longer-term relationship.

The business of automotive sales is a dynamic field, and to stay ahead, embracing change is essential. The trend now is clear: Collaborative negotiations, underpinned by genuine listening, are the future. Not only do they lead to more successful sales outcomes, but they also pave the way for lasting, positive relationships with customers.

Conclusion

In the high-octane world of car sales, where stakes are high and every conversation can make or break a deal, the subtle act of listening emerges as a potent tool. It redefines negotiations, turning them from mere deals to genuine relationships.

To reiterate the enduring wisdom of Dean Rusk, whether you're brokering international treaties or guiding a customer in a showroom, the art of listening, truly and genuinely, is perhaps the most potent persuasive tool at your disposal.

Goals:

1. Recognize listening as a crucial tool in successful negotiations.
2. Understand the emotions and motivations driving the other party.
3. Use listening to find common ground and build win-win situations.
4. Uncover hidden objections or concerns through attentive listening.
5. Strengthen negotiation outcomes through mutual understanding.

Prompts:

1. Think of a successful negotiation you were part of. How did listening play a role?
2. How do you ensure you're truly understanding the other party's viewpoint during a negotiation?
3. Can you recall a negotiation that failed due to a lack of understanding?
4. How do you handle emotionally charged negotiations?
5. How often do you use listening to steer negotiations towards win-win outcomes?

Reflections:

1. Every negotiation is an opportunity to create mutual value.
2. Emotions run high in negotiations, making listening even more crucial.
3. Finding common ground often starts with attentive listening.
4. Listening uncovers motivations, objections, and possibilities.
5. The best negotiators are often the best listeners.

CHAPTER TEN

CULTIVATING A LISTENING MINDSET:

EMBRACING CONTINUOUS GROWTH

In a world filled with the noise of constant information, the clamor of marketing messages, and the ever-present urge to 'sell,' mastering the art of listening can often be the silent game-changer. As we've navigated through this book, it's become evident that the ability to truly listen holds transformative power, especially for those in the automotive sales industry.

The shift from "always be closing" to "always be listening" is a monumental one, fundamentally altering the dynamics of a sales interaction. As Zig Ziglar stated, "You can get everything in life you want if you will just help enough other people get what they want." But how do we discern what others truly want? The answer lies in cultivating a listening mindset.

The Essence of a Listening Mindset

A listening mindset isn't merely about hearing words spoken; it's about tuning into the frequencies of emotion, motivation, and intent. Grant Cardone, a sales training guru and entrepreneur, noted, "There's no such thing as a good or bad economy; there's only the trained and untrained." In the realm of listening, the training we need isn't just of skills but of the mind itself.

The Path to Cultivating the Listening Mindset

1. **Self-awareness:** This is the starting point for any trans-formative journey. Recognize your triggers and behaviors when in a conversation. Are you preparing your response or truly understanding the speaker's emotions and underlying intentions? Journaling your feelings after a sale or using reflective practices can provide insights into your listening habits.

2. **Genuine Curiosity:** Brian Tracy mentions, "Become genuinely interested in other people." Instead of approaching a conversation as a means to an end, look at it as an exploration. Each person has a unique story, and your role is to uncover that narrative. By focusing on understanding their world, you organically frame better questions and gain clearer insights.

3. **Eliminate Prejudgment:** Over time, based on past experiences, salespeople tend to develop stereotypes or preconceived notions. While past experiences provide lessons, every client is unique. By being aware of these biases and actively challenging them, you open the door to unexpected opportunities and truly tailor your offerings.

4. **Mindful Presence:** Modern distractions, both digital and mental, can scatter our attention. The art of mindfulness, being wholly present in the moment, is invaluable in a sales context. Regular mindfulness exercises or meditation practices can help train your mind to stay anchored to the present, ensuring that you absorb every nuance of the customer's narrative.

5. **Active Feedback:** Instead of holding onto your thoughts or rebuttals, periodically offer feedback to the customer. This might look like summarizing what they've said or seeking clarifications. Not only does this enhance under-

standing, but it also reinforces to the customer that they are genuinely being heard.

6. **Continuous Learning:** Just as the automotive industry evolves, so do the tools and techniques for effective listening. Engage in regular training, be it workshops, courses, or reading materials, to refine and expand your listening capabilities.

Reaping the Rewards: A Listening Mindset in Action

Imagine an automotive sales interaction where the customer is a young parent looking for a family car. By practicing genuine listening, you uncover more profound needs and desires, leading to tailored presentations and, consequently, more sales.

The Ripple Effect: Beyond Immediate Sales

The long-term benefits of a listening mindset, from attracting repeat customers to positive word-of-mouth, can often surpass the value of any single transaction.

Conclusion: The Symphony of Sales Success

In the fast-paced world of automotive sales, it's the silent power of listening that often makes the loudest impact. By cultivating a listening mindset, you unlock the potential to not just sell but to form lasting relationships, and therein lies the essence of true sales success.

Goals:

1. Understand the long-term benefits of a listening mindset.
2. Recognize and challenge existing biases and preconceived notions.
3. Integrate mindfulness techniques to enhance listening capabilities.
4. Prioritize continuous learning to refine listening skills.
5. Transition from "always be closing" to "always be listening."

Prompts:

1. How has your mindset about listening evolved over your career?
2. What biases do you recognize in yourself that might hamper genuine listening?
3. How often do you engage in mindfulness or other practices to enhance your listening?
4. What resources or techniques do you use to continuously refine your listening skills?
5. Can you envision a sales environment where "always be listening" is the primary motto?

Reflections:

1. Mindset shapes actions, and a listening mindset shapes successful interactions.
2. Every preconceived notion I shed opens the door for a more genuine connection.
3. Mindfulness not only enhances my listening but enriches my life.
4. Continuous learning is the key to being a master listener.
5. "Always be listening" might be the mantra that redefines my sales career.

CHAPTER ELEVEN

STORYTELLING AND SALES: LISTENING TO CRAFT A NARRATIVE

In the words of Philip Pullman, "After nourishment, shelter, and companionship, stories are the thing we need most in the world." This profound thought isn't limited to books or films; it very much applies to the world of sales. In a marketplace saturated with choice, how can a salesperson make a product stand out? The answer lies in storytelling. And as you might expect, good storytelling starts with great listening.

Why Stories Matter

Stories are as ancient as human civilization. They have always been our primary tool to convey information, emotions, and values. Stories have an unparalleled power to engage the human mind, creating an emotional connection that raw data and facts cannot. As Jonathan Gottschall puts it in *The Storytelling Animal,* humans are, by nature, "storytelling animals." He explains, "We are, as a species, addicted to story. Even when the body goes to sleep, the mind stays up all night, telling itself stories."

When applied to sales, particularly in automotive sales, crafting a narrative around a car isn't about recounting its specifications or listing its features. It's about fitting the vehicle into the buyer's life story, showing them how it complements their aspirations, solves their problems, and elevates their status.

The Role of Listening

Before crafting a compelling narrative, one must gather the elements to build it. Here, listening becomes the primary tool. Maya Angelou once said, "People will forget what you said, people will forget what you did, but people will never forget how you made them feel." By listening intently to a potential car buyer, you collect the emotional, practical, and aspirational aspects of their life. These elements form the building blocks of your narrative.

Now, consider a real-life scenario. A young couple walks into the showroom, expecting their first child. They mention their excitement, their preparation for the baby's room, and their current car's inadequacy for a growing family. Now, an ordinary salesperson might just show them family cars within their budget. But a storyteller will do something different

Crafting the Narrative

From listening to the couple, the salesperson learns about their anticipation and the lifestyle changes they're about to undergo. The narrative then becomes about a safe and comfortable car that caters to a new family. The salesperson might say, "Imagine the first time you bring your baby home. As you securely place the car seat in the back, you'll know that this car, with its top safety ratings, will protect your most precious cargo. And as your family grows, the spaciousness will accommodate every little adventure you plan."

Such a personalized story speaks directly to the couple's heart. It's not just about the car anymore; it's about their journey as a family.

Benefits of Storytelling in Sales

1. **Emotional Connection:** By crafting a story that resonates with the buyer's personal experiences and aspirations, you form a bond that goes beyond the transactional. It's about shared values and understanding.
2. **Memorability:** As Chip and Dan Heath mention in their book *Made to Stick*, stories are inherently sticky. They stay with us long after dry facts have faded. A customer might forget a car's exact horsepower or mileage, but they'll remember the story of how it fits into their life.
3. **Overcoming Objections:** A well-crafted narrative anticipates and addresses potential objections. By painting a vivid picture of the benefits, objections like price or fuel efficiency become secondary to the overall experience.
4. **Word of Mouth:** Stories are shared. When a customer feels they've bought not just a car, but a story, they're more likely to share their experience, driving referrals.

Conclusion

In *Secrets of Closing the Sale*, Zig Ziglar asserts, "People don't buy for logical reasons. They buy for emotional reasons." By marrying the art of storytelling with the skill of listening, automotive salespeople can create compelling narratives that speak to those emotions. In doing so, they don't just sell cars; they sell experiences, dreams, and aspirations. In a world where customers are bombarded with choices, a good story, born from attentive listening, can make all the difference.

Goals:

1. Understand the significance of storytelling in the sales process.

2. Learn to craft personalized stories from customer conversations.
3. Identify key elements that make a narrative engaging and relatable.
4. Recognize moments in conversation to insert a relevant story.
5. Become skilled in using stories as tools to handle objections.

Prompts:

1. Think of a time when a story influenced your decision. What made it impactful?
2. Which elements of a story usually captivate your attention the most?
3. How often do you share personal anecdotes with your customers?
4. Recall a situation where a story helped you build rapport with a client.
5. How can you use storytelling to emphasize the value of a product or service?

Reflections:

1. How has integrating storytelling into your sales technique affected customer engagement?
2. What feedback have you received from clients about your stories?
3. How have your storytelling skills evolved over time?
4. Which stories resonate most with customers and why?
5. Are there situations where a story may not be appropriate?

CHAPTER TWELVE

TRADE-INS AND UPGRADES: LISTENING TO EVOLVING NEEDS

Before diving deep into the intricacies of empathetic listening in the realm of trade-ins and upgrades, let's begin with the story of James, a seasoned automotive salesperson, who once had a significant experience that changed his approach towards customers and their trade-ins forever.

James was known in his dealership for being a top performer, always ahead in numbers, but there was something that often eluded him—lasting relationships with clients. He followed the script, making sure to hit all the right notes and closing deals, but he felt something was missing.

One sunny afternoon, a customer named Clark walked into the dealership. Clark, a middle-aged gentleman, was there to trade in his old sedan for an upgrade. James, spotting an opportunity, quickly approached Clark and began his rehearsed speech about the latest models and their features. However, Clark interrupted him, pointing towards his old sedan and said, "That car holds a lot of memories. I'm not just here to trade in a vehicle. I'm moving on from a significant phase of my life."

James, instead of reverting to his standard pitch, decided to take a different approach. He invited Clark to sit down and asked him, "Would you like to share some memories associated with your old car?" Clark hesitated initially but then began recounting tales of family road trips, his daughter's first drive, and even the time when the sedan was their home during a camping trip that went awry.

As Clark shared his stories, James truly listened. He began to understand Clark's emotional attachment to the car and the gravity of the decision he was about to make. Instead of pushing the latest model, James asked Clark about the features he cherished in his old sedan and what he wished was better. Using this information, James suggested a model that retained the qualities Clark loved while offering upgrades on the aspects he felt were lacking.

Grateful for the genuine attention and personalized recommendation, Clark not only went ahead with the purchase but also became one of James' most loyal customers, often referring friends and family to him.

This experience was a revelation for James. He realized that by genuinely listening and understanding the deep-seated emotions and needs tied to a trade-in, he could foster lasting relationships, enhancing not just immediate sales but ensuring future ones through referrals and repeat business.

By infusing the narrative with this scenario, James becomes a conduit through which we understand the profound impact of empathetic listening in the world of automotive sales, particularly when dealing with trade-ins and upgrades. The scenario accentuates the significance of approaching each customer as an individual with unique stories, sentiments, and requirements.

For many consumers, automobiles are not just pieces of machinery. They're a testament to memories created, distances traveled, and chapters of life journeyed. In the realm of automotive sales, few situations are more-rife with emotion than the contemplation of a trade-in or an upgrade. It is at this juncture that empathetic listening becomes an invaluable tool for the salesperson.

The Emotional Anatomy of a Car Owner

Deep within the fibers of every vehicle lies a story, a narrative built over years of ownership. Whether it's the scratches on the bumper, reminiscent of a family vacation gone hilariously awry, or the faint coffee stain on the passenger seat from countless morning commutes, every car has its tales to tell.

Dale Carnegie once said, "When dealing with people, remember you are not dealing with creatures of logic, but with creatures of emotion." This couldn't be truer in the context of automotive trade-ins and upgrades. To navigate these waters effectively, a salesperson must tap into a reservoir of empathy, paying heed to not just the spoken word but the emotional subtext that accompanies it.

Delving Deeper into the Case of James

Earlier, we introduced James, a middle-aged man sentimentally attached to his sedan of a decade. But let's delve deeper into his psyche. James remembers the day he brought his newborn daughter home from the hospital in that car, the time he hurriedly drove his wife to the ER in the dead of the night, and the evening drives he took to clear his mind. To him, this car isn't just an automobile; it's an archive of cherished memories.

But James also realizes that his sedan, showing its age, isn't as reliable as it once was. He's concerned about safety features, fuel efficiency, and technological advancements. The challenge for the salesperson is to balance James's emotional attachment to his current vehicle with the logical arguments for an upgrade.

Beyond the Obvious: The Art of Probing

Empathetic listening is about peeling back the layers of a conversation, seeking deeper understanding. It's about discerning the
said from the unsaid. When discussing trade-ins, instead of directly inquiring about the features a customer is seeking in a new
car, why not start by understanding what they loved most about
their old one?

For example, if a customer loved the sunroof in their old car because it reminded them of summer drives along the coast, the
salesperson can highlight similar features in newer models,
painting a picture of new memories waiting to be made.

Trade-Ins as Opportunities

Trade-ins are not just transactions; they're opportunities. They
present a chance to address evolving needs and to build upon the
narrative of the customer. By presenting trade-ins as a continua-
tion of the customer's story rather than an end, salespeople can
alleviate some of the emotional hesitance associated with the
process.

Empathetic Listening in the Digital Age

In today's interconnected world, salespeople often interact with
customers through digital channels before meeting in person.
Even in these digital interactions, empathetic listening is paramount. Emails, chats, or virtual meetings can still offer cues. The
way a customer describes their car, the memories they choose to
share, or even their concerns about a new purchase can offer a
wealth of information.

Harnessing the Power of Stories

May I remind you of what Zig Ziglar wrote about creating emotion, "People don't buy for logical reasons. They buy for emotional reasons." By collecting and internalizing stories from various customers, a salesperson can become a master storyteller, weaving these narratives into future sales pitches. Imagine telling a hesitant customer about another who had similar reservations but found joy in the decision to upgrade. This creates a sense of camaraderie and reassurance.

Incorporating Feedback

Feedback is a goldmine. After a successful trade-in or upgrade, solicit feedback. What made the customer decide to go ahead with it? What were their concerns? How did they feel post-purchase? This feedback, when listened to empathetically, can be used to refine future interactions.

Conclusion

Every successful sale, at its core, is a harmonious blend of logic and emotion. As salespeople in the automotive industry approach the nuanced topic of trade-ins and upgrades, their ability to listen —truly listen—becomes their most potent tool. By respecting the emotional journey of the customer while addressing their evolving practical needs, they can turn potential transactions into memorable experiences.

To paraphrase Maya Angelou, customers may forget the specifics of a deal, but they'll never forget how a salesperson made them feel. In the realm of trade-ins and upgrades, emotions run deep, and the power of empathetic listening becomes the bridge to trust, loyalty, and sustained success.

Goals:

1. Enhance understanding of the customer's motivations for trade-ins and upgrades.
2. Learn to ask the right questions to uncover the true value a customer sees in their current vehicle.
3. Recognize the signs of a potential upgrade or trade-in opportunity.
4. Develop strategies for presenting new vehicle options based on customer feedback.
5. Foster trust through transparency in discussing trade-in values.

Prompts:

1. What do you believe are the main reasons customers choose to trade in their vehicles?
2. How do you currently handle trade-in conversations?
3. Recall a recent trade-in discussion. Did you feel you understood the customer's needs completely?
4. How do you ensure that the customer feels valued during a trade-in conversation?
5. How can you better use listening to guide a trade-in conversation?

Reflections:

1. How has empathetic listening impacted your trade-in and upgrade conversations?
2. What has been your biggest learning in handling trade-ins?
3. How do you ensure customers leave satisfied, even if they get a trade-in value lower than expected?

4. How has active listening affected your upgrade sales figures?

5. How can you further refine your approach to trade-ins and upgrades?

CHAPTER THIRTEEN

BRIDGING THE GENERATION GAP:

LISTENING ACROSS AGES

George Bernard Shaw wisely noted, "The single biggest problem in communication is the illusion that it has taken place." This statement rings especially true when we talk about conversations across different age groups. In the car showroom, salespeople meet Baby Boomers, Gen Xers, Millennials, and Gen Zers, all coming with their unique set of expectations and experiences.

Diverse Ages, Diverse Needs

Imagine two customers at a dealership: Sarah, fresh out of college and eager to buy her first car, and Tom, in his 70s, looking for a more comfortable ride to replace his old vehicle. Both meet Mike, a salesperson skilled in listening and understanding.

1. **Tom's Interaction:** Mike didn't just see an older man; he saw an individual with specific needs. By asking questions and truly listening, Mike learned about Tom's weekend trips with family, his love for classic tunes, and his parking struggles in the city. This led Mike to suggest a car equipped with modern parking technology and a quality sound system. Tom walked away feeling genuinely understood.

2. **Sarah's Interaction:** Mike, instead of only showcasing the newest cars, listened to Sarah's priorities. She wanted safety, good gas mileage, and smartphone compatibility. Mike guided her to a vehicle that checked all those boxes, thanks to his patient listening.

Understanding Generational Preferences

Empathetic listening involves truly understanding the emotions and perspectives of the speaker. When applied to car sales, it can make a vast difference, especially considering the varied preferences of each generation. Here's how empathetic listening can help cater to the needs of different age groups:

Baby Boomers (Born 1946-1964): Boomers often value direct communication and personal interactions. When discussing options, use empathetic listening to truly grasp their concerns and needs. Maybe they're looking for a car that reminds them of a model they once loved or one that's safe for grandkids. By genuinely understanding their nostalgic connections or safety concerns, you can recommend a car that matches their needs and heart's desires.

Gen Xers (Born 1965-1980): This generation tends to appreciate a mix of traditional values and modern conveniences. They might be juggling between work, kids, and aging parents. Using empathetic listening, tune into their current life challenges. Are they needing a reliable car for family trips or something fuel-efficient for long commutes? By focusing on their expressed life situations, you can guide them toward a choice that's both practical and fulfilling.

Millennials (Born 1981-1996): Digital and environmentally conscious, Millennials often come prepared with their research. Instead of overloading them with information, use empathetic listening to identify gaps in their knowledge or understand their primary concerns. Are they looking for an eco-friendly option due to environmental concerns or a vehicle compatible with their tech devices? By listening deeply, you can tailor your approach to align with their values and provide information they might not have come across.

Gen Zers (Born 1997 and later): Fully integrated with tech, Gen Zers are not just looking for a car; they're seeking an experience. Listen carefully to their expectations and aspirations. Are they looking for the latest tech innovations or maybe a brand that aligns with their ethical views? By practicing empathetic listening, you can delve deeper into their world, helping them find a car that's not just a mode of transport but an extension of their personality.

To truly cater to each generation's unique needs, it's crucial not only to know the general preferences but to actively and empathetically listen to each individual. Remember, every buyer, regardless of age, wants to be heard, understood, and respected. By using empathetic listening, you not only meet their car needs but also build lasting relationships and trust.

Listening: The Key to Successful Sales

To navigate these generational differences in the sales world, here are some essential strategies centered on listening:

1. **Ditch Assumptions**: As Mike showed with Tom and Sarah, it's crucial not to stereotype based on age. Every customer is an individual.
2. **Craft the Right Message**: Drawing inspiration from Malcolm Gladwell's *Blink,* it's essential to remember we sometimes jump to conclusions without all the facts. Instead of a one-size-fits-all pitch, mold your message to the customer in front of you.

3. **Build Genuine Connections**: Dale Carnegie's timeless wisdom from *How to Win Friends and Influence People* rings true here: genuine interest in others goes a long way. By truly understanding each customer, regardless of their generation, you create trust.

Conclusion

While the landscape of automotive sales continuously evolves with new models, technologies, and marketing strategies, the essence of successful salesmanship remains anchored in one fundamental skill: listening. As we've journeyed through the generational preferences, from Baby Boomers to Gen Zers, it becomes evident that each era brings its unique set of values, experiences, and expectations. But beneath these differences lies a universal human desire: the longing to be genuinely understood.

For the automotive salesperson, this realization is golden. No amount of product knowledge or sales tactics can replace the genuine connection formed when a customer feels truly heard. It's in those moments of deep understanding that trust is forged, and trust, in the world of sales, is the bridge to successful transactions and lasting relationships.

Consider the benefits: by actively practicing empathetic listening, you're not just selling a car. You're creating an experience, shaping memories, and potentially influencing a customer's choices for years to come. Think of the young family looking for their first minivan, the retiree seeking a reliable car for leisurely drives, or the environmentally conscious young adult searching for a green vehicle. Each of these individuals, regardless of their age or background, seeks validation of their concerns and aspirations. By tuning in, asking the right questions, and truly absorbing their responses, you elevate the sales conversation from a mere transaction to a meaningful interaction.

In the competitive world of car sales, where multiple dealerships vie for a customer's attention with discounts, promotions, and flashy advertisements, setting oneself apart might seem challenging. However, the key differentiator often isn't just the price point or the range of models available. It's the sales experience. And central to this experience is the act of listening.

Let's circle back to George Bernard Shaw's insight: "The single biggest problem in communication is the illusion that it has taken place." In car sales, eliminating this illusion becomes pivotal. By ensuring that communication is genuine, two-sided, and steeped in understanding, you not only bridge the generational divides but also lay the foundation for a thriving, customer-centric business. After all, as Bryant A. McGill wisely pointed out, truly listening to another person is one of the most sincere forms of respect. In sales and in life, this respect can pave the way for countless opportunities and fruitful connections.

Goals:

1. Understand the varied expectations of different generational cohorts.
2. Learn to tailor conversations based on generational cues.
3. Recognize the importance of non-verbal communication across generations.
4. Become adept at bridging communication gaps with customers from different age groups.
5. Value the unique perspectives each generation brings to the buying experience.

Prompts:

1. How do you currently differentiate your sales approach for younger versus older clients?
2. Think about a time when a generational gap made a sale challenging. How did you navigate it?
3. How do you ensure you're keeping up with the changing preferences of different age groups?
4. Recall an instance where understanding generational differences positively influenced a sale.
5. What generational cues do you believe are vital for automotive sales?

Reflections:

1. How has recognizing generational differences improved your rapport with clients?
2. In what ways has your sales approach evolved by listening to different age groups?
3. How do generational preferences influence your vehicle presentation choices?
4. Which generation do you find the most challenging to connect with and why?
5. What additional resources could aid in understanding varied generational needs?

CHAPTER FOURTEEN

WORD TRACKS VS. AUTHENTIC DIALOGUE

The landscape of sales, especially in the automobile sector, has seen many shifts. However, in an age of informed consumers seeking genuine interactions, the emphasis on authentic dialogue has never been stronger. This chapter dives into the transformative nature of authentic conversations and the profound impact of empathetic listening in the world of car sales.

Historical Backdrop: The Era of Word Tracks

In the past, the sales domain leaned heavily on word tracks or scripted pitches. These were crafted to offer a uniform sales message to every customer, aiming to make each one feel valued and addressed. Yet, as Dale Carnegie insightfully pointed out, the key is to "always make the other person feel important." Overreliance on scripted interactions often missed this mark, treating customers as mere numbers rather than individuals.

The Challenges of Scripted Conversations

1. **Predictability:** Modern car buyers, equipped with a plethora of information, can easily identify scripted interactions. Such realizations often lead to disinterest or mistrust, as scripted pitches feel inauthentic.
2. **Inflexibility:** Every customer's need is distinct. A fixed script can't cater to these varying needs, making interactions feel forced and unnatural.
3. **Loss of Personal Touch:** Car sales, like any other sales domain, thrives on the foundation of relationships. Relying on predefined scripts can prevent genuine connections from forming.

The Gift of Genuine Connection

The world of automotive sales, like many other domains, thrives on connections. While the underlying product might be a vehicle, what truly drives a successful sale is the relationship cultivated between the salesperson and the customer. It's a dance of genuine interaction, where both parties engage in a shared journey of discovery, ultimately leading to mutual satisfaction.

The Power of Storytelling: My Personal Experience

One of my most memorable experiences at the dealership encapsulates the essence of genuine connection. On a Sunday afternoon, a couple entered our showroom. Their intent was clear: to purchase a car for their son, who was soon heading off to college. Now, in scenarios like this, it's tempting to dive straight into the specifications, features, or ongoing promotions. However, that day, something nudged me to take a different route.

Instead of launching into a sales pitch, I started by asking about their son. What was he studying? What were his hobbies? How did they feel about this new chapter in his life? As they shared, I listened—genuinely listened. Their pride in their son's achievements, their mixed feelings of excitement and apprehension about him leaving home, all poured out.

This conversation did more than just fill time; it allowed me to step into their shoes, to truly understand their needs and concerns. I realized they weren't just looking for a car; they were searching for reliability, safety, and a sense of security for their child who was soon venturing into the world.

With this newfound insight, backed by empathetic listening, my approach to the sale became more tailored. Instead of showcasing the latest sports model, I steered them toward a vehicle known for its safety ratings, fuel efficiency, and longevity. I highlighted features that would benefit a young college student, such as integrated GPS for those trips back home and a sound system that would be the envy of his friends.

As we wrapped up, the father confessed something profound. He said, "Today, you didn't just sell us a car. You provided peace of mind for two worried parents. Thank you for truly listening to us."

By the time the paperwork was being finalized, it felt less like a transaction and more like the culmination of a shared experience. This sale was not the result of a rehearsed pitch but stemmed from genuine interaction rooted in empathetic listening. I didn't just understand their need; I felt it. And that connection, that genuine bond, made all the difference.

In the realm of car sales, vehicles might be the tangible product, but the intangible bonds forged, based on trust and understanding, are what truly drive success.

Embracing Authentic Conversations

True conversations are not just about completing a sale. They are centered around truly listening to and understanding the customer's specific needs and wants. When you take the time to actively engage in such a conversation, you move away from scripted interactions and step into a more authentic dialogue tailored to each customer.

Ralph Waldo Emerson once said, "The need to understand and be understood is fundamental." This idea is especially relevant in car sales. For many people, buying a car isn't just about getting a vehicle. It's about achieving goals, marking significant life events, or fulfilling long-held dreams.

When selling cars, it's essential to remember that behind every purchase decision is a story or a reason. Maybe it's a new job, the birth of a child, a long-anticipated road trip, or simply the culmination of years of saving. By genuinely listening to the customer, you can tap into that story, making the buying process more personal and meaningful.

To truly "always be listening," the focus should be on asking open-ended questions and paying close attention to the customer's responses. It's not about listening to reply with a rehearsed word track, but about aligning what you offer with what the customer genuinely needs and values.

In the end, when you prioritize authentic conversations in car sales, you not only foster trust and loyalty but also ensure that each sale is a reflection of the customer's unique journey and aspirations.

Empathetic Listening: The Pillar of Authentic Dialogue

At the heart of any meaningful conversation lies the ability to listen with empathy. Instead of just catching the words, it's about grasping the deeper sentiments and emotions they convey. For a salesperson, this form of listening is crucial. It ensures that customers feel genuinely heard and understood.

Grant Cardone put it simply: "Selling is about finding out what someone wants and delivering it." This wisdom underscores the power of truly hearing a customer. When we actively and empathetically listen, we move beyond just the surface. We delve into what drives the customer, what they genuinely desire, and what their concerns might be.

In the context of car sales, this means going beyond the standard features of a vehicle. It's about discovering why a customer is in the market for a new car. Are they looking for safety because they have a new family member? Do they need something reliable for a new job? Or maybe they want to celebrate a personal achievement with a new ride. By embracing empathetic listening, salespeople can tailor their approach to each unique story, making the buying process more personalized and ensuring the customer's needs are truly met.

While word tracks might offer a safety net for new salespeople, they're not the path to long-term success. To truly thrive in car sales, one must embrace authentic dialogue, understanding that real connections, built on trust and understanding, are the keys to sealing the deal.

The Evolution: From Scripts to Authenticity

It's clear that the days of relying on word tracks in car sales are behind us. The modern car buyer seeks a consultative approach, where the salesperson plays the role of a trusted advisor, guiding the customer based on their unique needs and desires. The emphasis is on listening, understanding, and then offering solutions, rather than pushing a predetermined pitch.

Conclusion

The journey of car sales has transitioned from the confines of rehearsed scripts to the expansive realm of authentic dialogue. The crux lies in the principle of "always be listening." By anchoring interactions in empathetic listening and genuine concern, salespeople not only meet the immediate needs of the customer but also lay the foundation for lasting relationships and continued success.

Goals:

1. Understand the importance of authentic dialogue in sales conversations.
2. Recognize situations where word tracks can hinder rapport-building.
3. Learn to seamlessly merge scripted responses with genuine interaction.
4. Appreciate the value of authenticity in long-term customer relationships.
5. Become adept at reading situations to decide between scripts and spontaneous dialogue.

Prompts:

1. How often do you rely on word tracks during sales conversations?
2. Recall a situation where a scripted response felt out of place. How did you pivot?
3. Think about a recent genuine dialogue with a client. What was the outcome?
4. How do you maintain authenticity while ensuring you cover essential sales points?
5. What barriers do you face in shifting from word tracks to authentic dialogue?

Reflections:

1. How has integrating more authentic dialogue affected your sales outcomes?
2. What feedback have you received from clients about your interaction style?
3. In which scenarios did word tracks prove beneficial?
4. How have you balanced authenticity with professionalism?
5. How do you plan to further enhance the genuineness of your interactions?

CHAPTER FIFTEEN

THE FIRST IMPRESSION - SETTING THE STAGE WITH ATTENTIVE LISTENING

The saying, "You never get a second chance to make a first impression," is as old as it is true. In sales, where first impressions play a pivotal role, the significance of this adage cannot be overstated. This chapter delves deep into understanding the power of attentive listening in creating lasting first impressions, offering a roadmap to mastering this skill in the high-stakes world of automotive sales.

Historical Perspectives: The Legacy of First Impressions

From the time of ancient trade routes to modern-day showrooms, sales have been an integral part of human society. Throughout history, merchants and traders realized the importance of first impressions. Dale Carnegie, a figurehead in the world of interpersonal skills development, once noted, "The expression one wears on one's face is far more important than the clothes one wears on one's back." Indeed, the impact of first impressions can be traced back to our very evolution, with our ancestors needing to quickly assess if someone was a friend or foe.

The Neuroscience Behind First Impressions

To understand the significance of attentive listening in making a positive first impression, it's crucial to grasp the neuroscience behind it. Within seconds of meeting someone, the amygdala and posterior cingulate cortex parts of the brain are activated, evaluating trustworthiness and making rapid judgments. These judgments, once formed, are notoriously difficult to change.

Given this swift judgment mechanism, the initial moments of a sales interaction are paramount. Active, attentive listening during these moments signals respect, attentiveness, and genuine interest.

Dr. Julian Treasure, a renowned sound consultant, says, "Listening is our access to understanding. Conscious listening always creates understanding." For an automotive salesperson, this understanding lays the foundation for trust, rapport, and eventually, a successful sale.

The Pillars of Attentive Listening in First Encounters

1. **Non-Verbal Cues:** Over 70% of our communication is non-verbal. An attentive listener, therefore, pays heed to the customer's body language. Is their posture open or closed? Are their gestures animated or reserved? These cues offer invaluable insights into the customer's state of mind.
2. **Verbal Attentiveness**: This involves not just hearing the words but comprehending the meaning behind them. Asking clarifying questions or paraphrasing what the customer says reinforces that they are truly being listened to.

3. **Emotional Resonance**: An attentive listener taps into the emotions underlying the words. Is the customer excited about the new car or anxious about the financial commitment? Recognizing these emotions allows the salesperson to tailor their approach.

Case Study: The Attentive Listener's Triumph

Consider the story of Alex, an automotive salesperson. One day, a young couple walked into the showroom. Instead of launching into a rehearsed pitch, Alex took a moment to truly listen. He noticed the couple's excitement but also sensed an undercurrent of anxiety. By attentively listening to their concerns about safety features, owing to a recent accident, Alex was able to address them specifically, leading to a sale and two delighted customers.

Fine-Tuning the Art of Listening

Being an attentive listener requires continuous effort. It's not merely about the ears, but engaging one's entire being. Renowned sales expert Brian Tracy aptly noted, "The greatest gift you can give to someone is the purity of your attention." For automotive salespeople, honing the art of attentive listening can involve:

1. **Role-playing**: Practicing with colleagues to simulate customer interactions can refine listening skills.
2. **Feedback**: Regular feedback from peers or mentors helps in identifying areas of improvement.
3. **Continuous Learning**: Engaging with resources, be it books or seminars on active listening, is invaluable.

The Undeniable Returns of Attentive Listening

The rewards of attentive listening, especially in the realm of first impressions, are manifold:

1. **Higher Sales Closure Rates:** By understanding the customer's true needs right from the outset, salespeople can offer tailored solutions, increasing the likelihood of a sale.
2. **Building Trust:** Customers are more likely to trust salespeople who they believe have their best interests at heart.
3. **Referrals:** A positive first impression not only seals a sale but also makes it likely that the customer will refer friends or family.

Conclusion:

The world of automotive sales is intricate, with multiple facets at play. Yet, amidst all the strategies, tactics, and techniques, the age-old wisdom of attentive listening stands tall. By mastering this art, especially in the critical initial interactions, salespeople set the stage for success, building a legacy of trust, rapport, and an ever-growing customer base. As they embark on this journey of continuous listening and learning, every first impression becomes a doorway to lasting relationships and soaring sales.

Goals:

1. Recognize the power of first impressions in shaping customer interactions.
2. Master the art of making customers feel heard from the first moment.
3. Understand the non-verbal cues essential in initial meetings.

4. Develop strategies to steer first conversations positively.

5. Ensure every initial interaction lays the foundation for trust.

Prompts:

1. Think back to a recent first interaction with a client. How did you ensure they felt heard?

2. How do you prepare mentally before meeting a potential customer for the first time?

3. Recall an instance where an initial interaction didn't go as planned. What would you change?

4. What non-verbal cues do you believe are critical in the first few minutes of a conversation?

5. How do you ensure you're completely present during initial interactions?

Reflections:

1. How have your first impressions influenced the trajectory of a sale?

2. What has been the feedback from clients about their initial meetings with you?

3. How do you recover if a first interaction doesn't go well?

4. How has attentive listening shaped your first impressions?

5. What additional strategies could further enhance your initial interactions?

CONCLUSION

We've journeyed together through the multifaceted world of listening, exploring its depth, its importance, and its techniques. This journey was embarked upon not just for the sake of understanding but to equip you, the automotive sales professional, with the tools and insights required to excel.

Transforming Old Paradigms

For many years, the stereotypical image of a car salesperson has been one of a slick talker, always having an answer, always pushing for a close. Yet, the dynamics of sales, especially in the automotive industry, have shifted. Customers today are more informed, have higher expectations, and seek genuine connections before making a purchase. The hard-sell techniques of yesteryear no longer hold the same weight.

In an illuminating observation, Daniel Pink, in his book *To Sell Is Human*, noted, "The ability to move others to exchange what they have for what we have is crucial to our survival and our happiness. It has helped our species evolve, lifting our ancestors out of their savage surroundings and into the light of civilization." Think about this in terms of empathetic listening. To truly move others, we must understand them, resonate with their needs and aspirations. This is where empathetic listening takes center stage.

Creating Lasting Impressions

One can argue that the first impression is crucial in a sale, but the lasting impression determines referrals, repeat business, and long-term customer loyalty. One of the most potent tools to create a lasting positive impression is by truly listening. Customers will often forget the exact words you said, but they'll always remember how you made them feel. When they feel heard, valued, and understood, they not only trust you more but also become more receptive to your guidance and suggestions.

Dr. John Gottman, a renowned relationship expert, once observed that "Emotionally intelligent couples are intimately familiar with each other's world." This holds true in sales as well. Knowing the intricate details of a customer's world, their needs, their desires, their fears, and their aspirations can position a salesperson not as a mere vendor but as a trusted advisor.

The Financial Benefits of Empathetic Listening

Empathetic listening isn't just a soft skill; it's a powerful tool that can directly impact the financial success of an individual automotive salesperson. Here's how mastering this invaluable skill can translate into tangible financial rewards for you, the automotive sales professional:

1. **Higher Commissions from Increased Sales**: When you truly understand a customer's desires, needs, and concerns, you're in a prime position to cater to them. This isn't about pushing a sale but about providing solutions. As you cultivate this understanding, you'll find that not only do you close more deals, but you also sell higher-value vehicles or packages, leading directly to higher commissions.

2. **Earn Repeat Business**: Repeat customers are the hallmark of a successful salesperson. If clients feel genuinely understood and cared for, they're far more likely to return to you for their next purchase, ensuring a continuous stream of revenue without the initial hard work of acquiring a new lead.

3. **Upselling and Cross-selling Potential**: By understanding the deeper needs and desires of your clients through empathetic listening, you're better positioned to suggest relevant add-ons, accessories, or even upgraded models. These aren't seen as pushy upsells but as informed recommendations, enhancing your earning potential.

4. **Fewer Returns or Cancellations**: Returns or canceled orders can be a significant setback, both in terms of commission and reputation. When you're attuned to your customer's true needs, the chances of post-purchase dissonance decrease, ensuring that your sales remain closed.

5. **Referrals Lead to More Sales**: A satisfied customer is the best marketing tool. Those who've had a positive experience with an empathetic salesperson are more likely to refer friends, family, or colleagues. These word-of-mouth referrals can significantly boost your clientele and, consequently, your earnings.

6. **Efficient and Effective Negotiations**: Being in tune with a customer's reservations or concerns allows you to address them proactively. This clarity can streamline negotiations, help close deals faster, and often at better terms, further boosting your commissions.

7. **Build a Strong Personal Brand**: In an industry as competitive as automotive sales, personal differentiation is vital. Being known as the salesperson who "truly listens and understands" can be a unique selling proposition, at-

tracting higher-quality leads and clients willing to pay premiums for personalized service.

8. **Reduced Stress and Greater Job Satisfaction**: There's undeniable satisfaction in knowing you've genuinely helped someone make the right decision. This fulfillment can reduce job-related stress and burnout, leading to a more extended, more profitable career.

9. **Quick Identification of Customer Needs**: Empathetic listening allows you to swiftly identify what the customer is looking for, reducing the time spent on pitches or presentations that don't align with their needs. This efficiency means you can attend to more clients, thereby increasing potential sales.

10. **Leveraging Ancillary Products and Services**: Beyond the vehicle itself, there's a plethora of additional products and services, from warranties to service packages. With a deep understanding of your customer's concerns and lifestyle, you can position these effectively, adding to your total sales volume.

To echo a thought by Jim Rohn, "If you just communicate, you can get by. But if you communicate skillfully, you can work miracles." For an automotive salesperson, this miracle is the consistent and substantial financial reward that comes from genuinely understanding and catering to the needs of each customer. In essence, as you prioritize listening, your commissions and overall earnings can see a remarkable uptick. Empathetic listening, therefore, is not just a good-to-have skill; it's the cornerstone of a lucrative career in automotive sales.

Empathetic Listening as a Lifelong Skill

The principles and techniques shared in this book aren't restricted to the realm of sales. They are life skills. Whether you're interacting with your family, friends, or strangers, the art of empathetic listening can enhance the quality of your relationships.

Ellen Hendriksen, in her book *How to Be Yourself*, states, "The opposite of speaking isn't listening. The opposite of speaking is waiting." The world today is full of individuals waiting for their turn to speak. By choosing to listen, you're not only distinguishing yourself professionally but personally as well.

Action Steps

1. **Practice, Practice, Practice:** Just understanding empathetic listening isn't enough. It requires daily, deliberate practice. Begin with small interactions, maybe with friends or family, and consciously apply the techniques discussed. Gradually, it'll become second nature.
2. **Seek Feedback**: Every interaction offers a lesson. After a sale, especially if it didn't convert, ask for feedback. Understand areas where you could've listened better or asked better questions.
3. **Continuous Learning**: The world of sales and human psychology is vast. There's always something new to learn, a technique to master. Commit to lifelong learning. Read books, attend seminars, and participate in workshops focused on sales, listening, and communication.
4. **Mentoring**: As you progress and see the fruits of empathetic listening, mentor junior salespeople. Share your experiences, your successes, and failures. This not only

positions you as a leader but also reinforces your learning.

5. **Self-Reflection**: Regularly take time to reflect on your interactions. Think about instances where you truly understood your customer and others where you might have jumped the gun. Analyze, understand, and learn from both.

In the words of Grant Cardone, "Your greatness is limited only by the investments you make in yourself." Empathetic listening is an investment, an investment that promises immense returns both professionally and personally. It's the pathway to not just selling cars but forging relationships, building trust, and establishing a legacy as a salesperson who truly understands.

Embrace this journey. Remember, in the orchestra of sales, while many instruments play, it's the quiet, profound notes of empathetic listening that often resonate the most. Be that note, be that difference.

In conclusion, empathetic listening is not just a tool for the modern salesperson; it is the very essence of effective selling. As you go forth, armed with the knowledge and insights from this book, remember that your greatest asset is not just your product or your pitch, but your ability to genuinely understand and connect with another human being. And in this connection, in this dance of emotions and needs, lies the true art of selling. Always be listening.

RESOURCES FOR YOUR CONTINUED SUCCESS

Congratulations on embarking on the transformative journey of *Always Be Listening: Supercharge Your Sales by Listening More & Closing Less*. To support your ongoing growth as an automotive sales professional and provide you with additional avenues for learning and inspiration, we've compiled a list of resources that complement the concepts and strategies discussed in this book. These resources will empower you to delve deeper into the art of attentive communication, enhance your sales skills, and connect with a dynamic community of like-minded professionals.

Online: Dave Ingland's Official Website at daveingland.com

Visit Dave Ingland's official website for access to a wealth of articles, online courses, blog posts, and resources dedicated to the world of automotive sales and attentive communication. Explore insightful content that delves into the intricacies of effective listening, rapport-building, customer understanding, and negotiation strategies. This online hub serves as a valuable repository of knowledge and guidance to help you live a happy life and achieve your goals.

YouTube: Dave Ingland's YouTube Channel at youtube.com/daveinglandmedia

Subscribe to Dave Ingland's YouTube channel for a visual and interactive learning experience. Access a collection of videos that offer practical tips, real-world examples, and engaging discussions on topics ranging from active listening techniques to customer-centric approaches in automotive sales. The channel is a valuable resource for visual learners seeking to enhance their sales expertise.

Podcast: "The Epic Sales Podcast" at redcircle.com/shows/epic-sales

Tune in to "The Epic Sales Podcast" hosted by Dave Ingland. Immerse yourself in insightful conversations with industry experts, thought leaders, and successful sales professionals. Gain exclusive insights into effective communication strategies, customer engagement tactics, and innovative approaches to increase sales and income while living a happy life. Each episode offers a unique perspective and practical advice to help you thrive in the competitive world of automotive sales.

Social Media Engagement:

Connect with Dave Ingland and fellow automotive sales professionals across various social media platforms. Join an active, nationwide community dedicated to sharing insights, success stories, and inspiration. Stay updated with the latest developments in our training and resource materials, and engage in meaningful discussions that foster continuous growth and learning.

- Facebook Group: facebook.com/groups/myepicsales
- Facebook Page: facebook.com/daveinglandmedia
- Instagram: instagram.com/daveingland.media
- TikTok: tiktok.com/@daveinglandmedia
- X (Formerly Twitter): twitter.com/daveinglandx

By becoming part of this vibrant community, you'll have the opportunity to exchange ideas, ask questions, and celebrate victories with fellow professionals who share your commitment to achieving their goals and having big dreams.

As you journey forward, remember that the path to success is a continuous one, marked by dedication, self-improvement, and the unwavering desire to learn and grow. We invite you to explore these resources and embrace the opportunity to evolve as a sales professional who prioritizes attentive communication, empathetic listening, and customer-centric interactions.

Thank you for choosing *Always Be Listening: Supercharge Your Sales by Listening More & Closing Less* as a companion in your quest for achieving your goals. May your journey be filled with discovery, transformation, and lasting success.